ISLANDS IN
THE STREAM

Islands in the Stream

Published by Four Wings Press in the United Kingdom 2023

Paperback ISBN: 978-1-7392638-0-5
Ebook ISBN: 978-1-7392638-1-2

Typeset in Adobe Garamond Pro, Calibri and Seabird SF by The Book Typesetters
Illustrations by Rebekah di Palma

ISLANDS IN THE STREAM

CLAIRE PASS AND RACHAEL BUSHBY

To all senior mental health leads, past, present and future,
who work with such passion and commitment.

Foreword

As Bushby and Pass emphasise, mental health and wellbeing are things we have to work at and strive for. Every part of society, every school community, every family in the land has its current challenges and wears the scars of battles past. And all of this *living*—the basic reality of who we are and where we've been—affects the mental health and wellbeing of all of us.

As I write this, my daughter is curled up next to me, battling a high fever. At work, I'm facing some tricky governance issues that risk tipping a high-pressure job into unhealthy levels of stress. In the background of my consciousness is the low hum of grief. I know I'm not alone. If we're honest, many of us are navigating the world through this kind of fog. And, as I know from my days at a mental health charity, this fog can thicken and become unnavigable without help.

One in four of us will experience a diagnosed mental health problem in our lifetime. Add in the fact—starkly described in this book—that the difficult circumstances we find ourselves in are also exacerbating factors for mental ill health—poverty, inequality, discrimination, abuse—and it is clear that good mental health practice has to be woven into the fabric of all of our public services.

Nowhere is this more important than in our schools. A staggering statistic in this book is that 50 percent of mental health problems are established by the age of 14. It is certain, following three years of disrupted schooling, and when children come to school hungry, or cold, that the caseload is set to rise.

But as Bushby and Pass highlight, the case for embracing positive approaches goes way beyond catching kids when they fall. Schools set our children up for life. If educators can embed the tools and practical action needed to promote wellbeing, and if teachers can role model self-care and openness, the benefit will be lifelong. It's like showing children where the fog lights are and how to turn them on. And for me—as someone who believes in social change—it is a means of rooting out stigma, by making talking about mental health the norm for every child in the land.

Which is why it is great news that the government is investing in mental health leadership in every school. But that's clearly not the end of it, because it's what senior mental health leads *do* that counts. And what Bushby and Pass have done is make the *doing* bit visible. Without prejudging any given SMHL's circumstances or any school's needs, this guide provides the framework to act strategically towards a more mentally healthy environment for teachers and pupils alike.

This book is clear that the going isn't always easy, and I wish SMHLs the best of luck with the critical work you do, as islands in the stream. Thank you for stepping up—you've never been more needed.

Anna Bird is CEO of a campaigning organisation in the not-for-profit sector and a passionate advocate for mental health and equality. She has led teams at Mind, Scope and the Fawcett Society, combining high ambition for social impact with an unrelenting focus on embedding a happy, healthy working culture. An academic background in mental health policy research, directing mental health policy for national charities, and being a busy working mum of two primary-aged children all fuel Anna's belief in the importance of early intervention for mental health, and the critical role schools can play in promoting wellbeing.

Contents

Introduction

If you asked a trainee teacher or teaching assistant why they chose the education profession, it is unlikely many would answer, 'To ensure pupils hone their exam technique across a breadth of subjects.'

Instead, they are more likely to respond that they want to make a difference, provide their pupils with the groundwork to live fulfilling and satisfying lives, or help young people to learn about and navigate our ever-changing world. People drawn to teaching environments instinctively know there is a bigger picture outside of academic achievement and that a flourishing life is nuanced.

After centuries of misinformation, misdiagnosis and mishandling, we are fortunate to live at a time when the stigma surrounding mental health is gradually being reduced. In the past decade, mental health is slowly being recognised as simply 'health', and the part played by senior mental health leads should not be underestimated.

At their apex, the senior mental health lead will support and aid the mental wellbeing and mental health of the ecosystem that is known as a school. They will prepare for the year ahead so that they can proactively assist in preventing future crises, which will leave them with the capacity to deal reactively to situations that require it.

But it can be a lonely role, even isolated. We have heard this time and again from the hundreds of senior mental health leads (SMHLs) we have trained. They are an island. And their position can be intensely challenging and demanding. When this isolation is mixed with other pressures, we might worry about the mental wellbeing of SMHLs.

That is why we decided to write this book—to stretch a hand across the water. To let you know that you are not alone and share the practical resources needed to deliver the role, while also building a community you can reach out to in return. This book has been written for everyone connected to the position, whether the head teacher deciding who to appoint, the seasoned SMHL or a newcomer, even someone who has not yet applied for the role. It will provide guidance and assistance at all stages and for all knowledge bases.

With that in mind, we firmly believe that many of the systems required to conduct the role are already in place in most schools, and the SMHL should begin by linking them up rather than starting from scratch. We are both teachers and have the best part of forty years of experience between us. We understand the pressures teaching professionals are under, the never-ending demands on your time and resources, the swinging (and sometimes lurching) changes in curriculum and targets. For that reason alone, we do not want to pile more onto your shoulders. What is the point of having you protect the mental health of others, if the position itself is detrimental to your own wellbeing? Instead, we want to pull a thread through the practices that already underpin your role. With a clear overview, you can acknowledge the gaps, and concentrate your efforts on them. It is often small, targeted adjustments that are the most impactful.

Although relatively new, the senior mental health lead's role is here to stay. It is not an initiative brought in by one government cabinet to be discarded by another. Nor will it fade away after it has been lauded as the 'new big thing' in education and then thoroughly debunked (we're talking about you, 'Learning Styles'). Instead, it is more akin to safeguarding, another potentially isolating role, but one that is so logical and necessary from our current perspective it is still strange to think that it only emerged as a priority in schools following major changes and the strengthening of legislation in the early 2000s.

There is another facet to an island we have not yet considered. Yes, it may appear isolated, but in the fast-flowing stream of the academic year, an island is a safe port for those in danger of sinking rather than sailing through the currents. An island also provides high ground, a vantage point from which the school can be surveyed. One that is essential to a cohesive, whole organisation approach to mental health.

So, why 'Islands in the Stream'? Not because we desired a catchy country tune to play through your mind (although in reading this sentence, it may have lodged there already). It is because we are both English teachers and although it is partly an esoteric nod to Hemingway, the real reason is our appreciation of the imagery. Our love of imagery also led us to name our organisation after the dragonfly. We admired their symbolism of growth, maturity, strength, bravery, joy and freedom. Having been around for over 350 million years, they know a thing or two about adapting to change and are the poster-insects for resilience. The imagery of an island in the stream similarly appealed to us. If the senior mental health lead is the island, the stream is a blend of the school's culture and society, with the current being the academic year.

This is where we will start, with the senior mental health lead in the landscape of the school culture, society and academic year; it will be the more reflective part of the book. In turn, this will help you adapt the advice in the second part of the book to your unique school setting. Then, in the second part, we dive deeply into the role itself, the tools needed to fulfil it, the scenarios you might face, the interventions that can be put in place, and ways to ensure the continuity and continuance of the role if a SMHL moves on.

But firstly, let's begin with the role itself. Because islands in our streams, that is what we are.

Claire Pass and Rachael Bushby
October 2022

Part One:
The Landscape

Chapter One: The Island

'It's useful to think about the pockets of good practice and how to unite them all under a whole school approach.'
– L.H. (SMHL, Cambridgeshire)

Most would agree that working in the education profession is much more encompassing than simply transferring academic knowledge from one mind to another. It is often a moral endeavour and, as educators, we feel responsible for the wellbeing of those in our care. Many schools and the people within them voluntarily take on roles of support far beyond the remit required of them. They do this because they see themselves as more than an educational institution—they are a stabilising presence, a family and occasionally even a refuge.

The irony is that there is very little in Initial Teacher Education that prepares us for this moral endeavour. During this time, we do not learn how to help others live a flourishing life or pass on effective and agile tools to nurture mental health. We are instead trained in pedagogical methods. Back when we both started teaching, no one spoke about the mental wellbeing of students. It was only acknowledged insofar as some children were labelled EBD (having emotional and behavioural difficulties) and were typically in the bottom sets. Not long after, a slow shift began, and there was a focus on the social and emotional aspects of learning but not of *living*.

More recently, some teacher educators have added rich offerings such as character education modules or mental health workshops, but these localised pockets of excellent professional development are not consistent. Consequently, many educators will say that their initial training has not prepared them for the moral responsibility of supporting children and young people with the inevitable challenges that come with 'life'.

So, when you are appointed to the senior mental health lead (SMHL) role, there can often be an overwhelming realisation that you now feel responsible for the mental health of numerous children and your colleagues. What many SMHLs do not realise, and what we are here to help with, is that many of the practices to promote good mental health are already in place. If you learn to evaluate the school's current position and where the gaps are, and focus your efforts on filling those gaps, the role will be transformed. We also have to be strategic, as opposed to having multiple people doing multiple tasks that don't connect and, as a result, don't have the desired impact.

We have trained hundreds of SMHLs to help them feel equipped, prepared, and excited about beginning the role. What is crucial for us is that the people we train can conduct the role in a sustainable way for them and their mental wellbeing. You don't need to be exhausted and burnt out in the pursuit of happiness for others, because that is detrimental and counterproductive on both personal and professional levels. We know that the research shows that staff wellbeing is directly connected to pupil wellbeing[1] and achievement.[2] Therefore, the first step is about choosing where to put your energies and bringing the school community on board with your vision about mental health provision. We show you how to join the dots between what is in place, letting go of some things that aren't working, and prioritising what we take forward, one step at a time.

A second key consideration is that this role must be sustainable because it is a vital and natural evolution from safeguarding. Many of us will remember a time when safeguarding wasn't what we know and respect in schools today. In our experience of working with schools nationwide, Designated Safeguarding Leads (DSLs) are now, without much deviation, well respected, well-trained, and well-suited to their role. The acknowledgement that safety is a key part of education means that the position of DSL has a status and a purpose that transcends the traditional, and rightly outdated, view that a school's sphere of influence is solely in the realm of outcomes such as exam results, sporting success or good manners. It is our sincere hope that the role of SMHL in your school has, or will have, the same status.

Lastly, even though we will show you how to streamline the processes in the following chapters to make it sustainable (and, dare we say, fulfilling and enjoyable), it should never be treated as a tick-box exercise. Any school that takes that view is missing an opportunity for a holistic approach to education that is needed to help students reach their full potential. The SMHL role celebrates and promotes what we already know—that education is not solely about the subjects covered in schools. Education is as far-reaching as the horizons of our lives, and mental health is a key component of that.

Mental health and education

After years of campaigning by non-governmental organisations, including Mind (and the amazing work of Time to Change), Rethink Mental Illness, the Centre for Mental Health, and the Mental Health Foundation, significant changes emerged in attitudes to mental health. Their work ensured mental health was treated on an equal footing with physical health and placed firmly on the government agenda in 2014 after the Department of Health published *Closing the Gap: Priorities for Essential Change in Mental Health* in January of that year.[3] The slogan 'Mental Health is Everybody's Business' was introduced to challenge the commonly held belief that some people were mentally ill or 'unstable', but for the majority, mental health wasn't an issue. The paper prompted the start of the integration of mental and physical health care to reinforce the message that 'mental health is health' and that we all have mental health, just as we all have physical health.

Any major shift in societal attitudes must include education, so schools and colleges were charged with promoting mental wellbeing to prevent mental health problems from developing. Just as schools were expected to teach children how to be physically healthy by extolling the benefits of getting enough exercise, eating nutritious food, and having sufficient sleep, they were now also expected to promote ways that children and young people could look after their mental health and wellbeing, which would, among others things, include exercise, nutritious food, and healthy sleep (some of the many dots already in place that the SMHL can begin to join).

Slowly, a national narrative shift began. Mental health went from being defined by lazy slang and images more befitting Victorian England to something that makes us 'normal' and human. Protests on social media challenged the sale of faux straightjackets as Halloween costumes, and we learned that one in four people will be diagnosed with a mental health condition in any given year.[4] There's still a way to go, and the stigma persists, but the movement is generally in a positive direction. Education really does make a difference.

Between 2016 and 2018, the Department for Education (DfE) conducted case studies of mental health provision in schools. The recommendations that emerged, along with seminal documents such as *Mental Health and Behaviour in Schools* published in 2018,[5] provided a base from which the role of the senior mental health lead took shape. Initially, the government wanted to start training a SMHL in every state-funded school in England in 2020. However, this was delayed by Covid-19. Post-Covid, the need has never been more apparent. By supplying funding for the training, the government's aim is to provide one person in each school with the knowledge and skills necessary to implement and lead a cohesive whole-school approach to mental health provision.

The government's agenda recognises that different areas face different challenges, so it is appropriate to respond to these at a local level, which aligns with our own vision of schools as the heart of communities. These local transformation plans and the desire to connect schools to local Mental Health Teams via the conduit of the senior mental health lead has left a new responsibility at every school's door, whether they are ready for it or not.

Key dates for mental health and education...

2014	Department of Health publishes *Closing the Gap: Priorities for Essential Change in Mental Health*
2016– 2018	Department of Education conducts case studies of mental health provisions in schools, leading to the recommendation of the SMHL role
2019	Ofsted incorporates mental health and mental wellbeing into its framework
2020	Training of a SMHL in every state-funded school in England to begin, which Covid-19 delays
2021	Funding for the training of a SMHL in every school is released
2025	Funding for training SMHLs is scheduled to end

Mental health, mental illness, and mental wellbeing

Before exploring the role of the SMHL, we must cover some crucial points that are fundamental to the position.

Mental health and mental illness are terms that are often wrongly used interchangeably. For years, some schools have only been reacting if they felt that there was a child who had an obvious mental illness. They would hopefully step in, signpost, and refer. But not all schools did the preventative and promotional work to create good mental wellbeing for all, whether that's people with mental health conditions or not. Slowly, it's becoming understood that there is a difference between mental health (which we all have) and mental illnesses (which some of us have, or might have, in the future). The inclusion of mental health in the 2020 PSHE guidance, making it compulsory for pupils to learn how to look after their mental wellbeing and recognise when classmates might be struggling, reflects this shift.

Even for us, working day in and day out with the subject, we find that the definitions are complex, controversial and ever-evolving. Phrases such as 'mental health is prevalent' are used all too regularly in the media and this perpetuates stigma and misunderstanding as it's like saying 'physical health is prevalent'. Here is how we define three key terms that the SMHL will need to be familiar with and use regularly:

Mental health refers to an objective view of a person's mood, thinking and behaviour (that can be measured using diagnostic tools). Everyone has mental health. Mental health includes cognitive and social skills, emotional regulation, empathy and flexibility, our ability to recover from adverse life events, and our capacity to thrive. It also encompasses mental wellbeing (see below). Our mental health is on a spectrum and fluctuates throughout life. Mental health is far broader than simply the absence of mental illness.

Mental wellbeing is a person's experience of the world and sense of self. It's subjective as it's about how they think and feel. It is therefore hard to measure accurately. Our mental wellbeing is part of our overall mental health. Low levels of mental wellbeing over prolonged periods make you more likely to develop mental ill health. And those with mental illness are more likely to experience low levels of mental wellbeing (but not always). At certain times, low levels of wellbeing are a mentally healthy response to a situation, such as grief.

Mental illness refers to a wide range of mental health conditions—disorders that affect your mood, the way you think, and the way you act. These have specific criteria and need to be diagnosed by a professional. Examples of mental illness include depression, anxiety disorders or schizophrenia. Mental illnesses can affect a person in the short-term or long-term. They are not always curable, but are always treatable.

A key step is to uncouple mental wellbeing (a very subjective concept) from mental health (a more objective concept defined by specific diagnostic measures). Although these terms are related, they are not synonymous. You can have a diagnosable, or even diagnosed, mental health condition and still have a good level of mental wellbeing. This can happen when everything you require to manage it is in place, be it medication, talking therapy, self-care, etc. People live decades with diagnosable mental illnesses but still have good mental wellbeing. Conversely, you might not have a diagnosable mental illness but have a low level of wellbeing because you are involved, for example, in a detrimental relationship or live in extreme poverty. In situations like these, mental wellbeing is impacted, not because of a diagnosable mental health condition but because of circumstances often outside of your control. Sometimes a low level of mental wellbeing is a completely apt response when you consider the person's overall situation.

There is an increasing understanding of the subtleties and nuances of terms like mental health and mental wellbeing and an appreciation that people's lives don't equate to labels. Our philosophy around mental health is a simple one—mental health and mental wellbeing are not simply defined by the absence of mental illness.

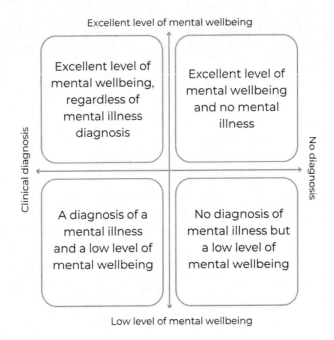

The role of the senior mental health lead

So, what is the role of the SMHL? If you read a relevant job description, you might see something akin to:

'This is a leadership role that includes oversight of all mental health provisions and interventions, education and training related to mental health and wellbeing and the development of spaces and resources to support mental health and wellbeing. The mental health lead will oversee how the school contributes to the promotion of good mental health and wellbeing for all members of the school community by:

- Developing a whole-school approach to mental health and wellbeing
- Effectively leading the school's mental health team
- Overseeing the effective implementation of the PSHE programme

- Gaining input from and establishing strong connections and working relationships with all stakeholders, community groups, and external agencies (e.g. CYPMHS)'

Another way of introducing it is to break down the key components of what the role is and, of equal importance, what it *isn't*:

The Senior Mental Health Lead is...

A leadership role to:

- Promote good mental health and emotional wellbeing among pupils and staff

- Develop a whole-school approach to support mental wellbeing

- Teach staff and pupils about mental health and mental wellbeing

- Play a key part in identifying emerging mental health needs of pupils and staff

- Ensure staff recognise signs and symptoms of mental health needs in pupils

- Implement a clear process to follow where a concern is raised about a pupil's mental wellbeing

- Develop links with specialist mental health services

- Signpost to pupils and families the local and national support available to them

- Refer pupils on to health professionals for appropriate support and treatment when required

> Support pupils identified as having mental health needs by ensuring staff are equipped with the skills required to aid students in their learning

The Senior Mental Health Lead isn't...

> A mental health professional

> Someone who diagnoses or treats mental health conditions

> Someone who will always have the answer

> Impervious to poor mental health

These duties can be summarised neatly into three strands:

- **promotion** (of good mental health),
- **prevention** (of poor mental health), and
- **early identification** (of those with mental health problems)

What is crucial to remember is that not all these things must be done by the SMHL. Instead, you *oversee* them as part of the strategic whole-school plan.

The term 'whole-school approach' is key. This is because so many roles in school are limited to a particular class, subject, or group. Whereas we need to include the entire system: all the staff, students, parents and carers, the governing board or trustees, the school's culture, and the surrounding community. We will be talking more about this in the next chapter.

The SMHL role is proactive as well as reactive. Desmond Tutu once said, *'There comes a point where we need to stop just pulling people out of the river. We need to go upstream and find out why they're falling in.'* As SMHLs, if we can travel further upstream and try to help prevent people from falling into mental ill health by promoting methods of protecting mental wellbeing, it is preferable to simply reacting when someone is flagged as having mental health needs. **Promotion** of good mental health and **prevention** of poor mental health is the proactive part of the role and can and should, wherever possible, be prepared in advance (more on this later). At the same time, **early identification** of those with mental health problems is often a combination of the proactive and reactive parts of the role.

The SMHL role also requires dexterous decision-making, alongside kindness and empathy, because when dealing with ethical questions, there isn't necessarily a right or wrong answer. Of course, there might be a distinctly wrong answer that we are sure you will avoid, such as repeatedly failing to refer to outside agencies when there is a clear and pressing need. But generally, these decisions are contextual and require moments of reflection to consider what is right for the staff and students within your community, considering the school culture, circumstances, what proceeded this and what's already in place. No matter how much paperwork you prepare, you will still be required to make difficult ethical decisions. We will discuss the different ways of approaching these dilemmas in Chapter 8.

To dip a toe into this and prepare for the scenarios that might arise as SMHL, consider the following:

Case Study

Billy is 11 and comes to school late most days. You are aware no one at home gets Billy up in the morning or is there to help him get ready for school, and there is no food in the house most of the time. Most nights Billy is awake until the early hours of the morning playing video games. Social care has been involved, but it never reached the stage of any intervention apart from monitoring.

When the school is able to contact mum, she says that Billy can't get out of bed in the morning because he's depressed. Billy has had several sessions with the school counsellor, and there have been improvements in his be-haviour, but the punctuality issue remains. Some other members of the form group have also started to be late (but on the surface, they don't seem to have the same challenges at home). When asked about it, they say that Billy always gets away with lateness.

The head of year wants to punish all the students with a day in isolation. Do you intervene to change the sanction for Billy?

For the moment, make a note of how you would approach this situation. You can then review this once you have read Chapter 8.

Who supports the SMHL?

Now that we have covered the scope of the role, we need to consider what a SMHL needs to manage it in a sustainable way. The answer to this is preparation and a whole-school approach.

The preparation side will be discussed in Chapter 4, but for now, let us consider the whole-school approach. Fundamentally, this means align-ing and involving the school community. But it also means, where pos-sible, forming a team internally and externally. Our ideal scenario, and the one we will help you work towards in the following chapters, is that you build a supportive team with whom you can discuss your approach to eth-ical dilemmas. This may be more difficult in a small primary school, but even if you can find one other person to discuss such problems with, it will be beneficial. Ideal potential candidates for this team are the head teacher, the DSL, the pastoral lead, or the heads of year. You are looking for people within the school who have a vested interest in shaping a positive mental health culture and want to be part of it.

When it comes to external support there are suggestions that we will cover more fully in Chapters 2 and 9, such as reaching out to the Mental

Health Support Team, if you have one in your local area, CYPMHS, and local organisations and charities such as Young Minds and Anna Freud. We also provide external support for SMHLs, and part of our aim for this book is to connect SMHLs across the country so that they are not islands working in isolation, but instead more like an archipelago with a community to rely upon.

For the moment, and before we begin the next chapter on school culture and society, take time for reflection. Consider how you envisage the landscape to look in the future when procedures are in place, the role is solidified and stable, and answer the following questions:

1. What already existing policies/procedures to promote mental wellbeing and support mental health did you align with your role as SMHL?
2. Who is on the team with you?
3. Which external agencies do you have a good working relationship with?
4. What innate qualities, skills, or experience did you bring to the role?
5. What skills or qualities do you need to work on mindfully now you are in this position?

Summary

✳ The senior mental health lead role is part of a societal shift to promote good mental wellbeing, open up dialogue and support on mental health.

✳ The role is relatively new, and the government aims to have one SMHL in each state-funded school in England by 2025.

✳ Mental health, mental wellbeing, and mental illness are related but not interchangeable terms.

✳ The SMHL role is to promote good mental health, work to prevent poor mental health and help with the early identification of those with mental health challenges.

✳ The role is a proactive and reactive one.

✳ The SMHL should not feel alone in their role within a school setting, and steps should be taken to bring in a whole-school approach to supporting the SMHL.

Chapter Two: The Stream

'I feel like a lot of this academic year has been about managing "crisis" and what comes through the door each day...I want to move from crisis intervention work, to create a whole school approach to mental wellbeing.'
– G.M. (SMHL, Merseyside)

Let us leave our island for the moment and travel upstream until we arrive close to its source. We are now at the confluence where the school culture and society meet. There may even be tension here, one washing over the banks of the other, but together these form the influences and setting we must understand to implement a whole-school approach.

Each child, with their individual background and experiences, flows into the school, which in turn has its own expectations and culture. It is the role of the school's leadership to blend these and the SMHL has an integral part to play here. This is because one of the most crucial aspects of mental health support, and what can make the difference for many young people, are the relationships they forge and the sense of belonging they feel as part of the school community.

For clarity, the importance of a whole-school approach stems in part from the document we mentioned in the previous chapter, *Mental Health and Behaviour in Schools*, published by the DfE in 2018. Among other things, it lists some protective factors for children's mental health. These include clear policies on behaviour and bullying, a whole-school approach to promoting good mental health, and good pupil-staff relationships. A whole-school system not only helps on a practical level, but also assists in the primary aim of the SMHL: to promote mental wellbeing and protect mental health.

A whole-school approach is also essential because a school needs a shared vision of what everyone is striving for. This allows for the proactive, preventative approach we discussed in the previous chapter. When staff work with clear expectations, know how to observe the signs of poor mental health, and have a transparent process to follow when concerns arise, schools can intervene early on. Ultimately, this means that many issues associated with poor mental health can be addressed before becoming a clinical need.

Whole-school approaches will vary depending on context, with the approach of an Alternative Provision school differing from an FE college. So how do we blend this mix of backgrounds, expectations, and approaches? First, as SMHL, we must understand the context of our inflow of pupils as this will, and should, help shape the culture within the school. If they are miles apart, this incongruence may give rise to a silent and insidious tension that over time negatively impacts the mental health of the pupils and even staff. It is therefore important that schools embrace the stories that children bring with them to the door. But equally, we don't want to perpetuate cycles of poverty or underachievement or ignore disaffected pupils. Second, we look at the school culture and consider how it might be enhanced to reflect and promote mental wellbeing and mental health.

Society

The attitudes, values and experiences of the pupils entering the school's doors are ultimately shaped by their society. We therefore used the term 'society' to encompass both the community that pupils come from and the attitudes, values, and experiences they carry into the school along with their school bags and equipment.

Why is this important? Because disadvantage, discrimination, physical ill health, a lack of family ties, and the broader interventions that children and young people might be going through, such as contact with the justice system or social services, all impact mental health and mental wellbeing. Unfortunately, certain populations are at higher risk of mental health problems because they are more vulnerable to unfavourable circumstances. Factors that impact people's mental health and drive inequality can include poor housing, unemployment, social injustice, immigration status, sexual orientation, gender identity, disabilities, ethnicity, experiencing violence or abuse and living in care. Of course, each pupil's individual lived experiences can be far-ranging and differ vastly from one another, but the SMHL should be aware of the aggravating factors that might be harming their mental health.

Some factors that impact mental health and mental wellbeing...

- Disadvantage

- Discrimination

- Marginalisation

- Inequality

- Physical ill health

- Lack of family ties

- Contact with the justice system

- Contact with social services

Suffering racial disparity, living with a disability, or belonging to the LGB-TQIA+ community, for example, might mean that you face marginalisation, additional barriers in life, inequality, and discrimination. It is important that the SMHL is comfortable acknowledging how elements of a person's identity interact with the aggravating factors listed, the intersectionality between these things, and the impact on mental health and wellbeing. Some people suffer low levels of mental wellbeing not because they have a mental illness, but because they live in circumstances that have provoked it, and their response is appropriate. We recently found a cartoon that captured the essence of this idea: a baby koala clings to a tree stump in a forest of felled trees, while two officials with clipboards stand over him, their backs to his environment. One says to the other, 'This young koala has a mental health problem.' In instances such as this, focusing solely on the individual koala as having 'a mental health problem' serves to diminish the appropriate response to difficult circumstances. It reduces the societal problem to an individual issue. It is therefore important to see the felled trees, acknowledge the trauma, and support the koala with compassion. Dr Caroline Johnson said we *'shouldn't pathologise normal reactions to abnormal circumstances.'*[6] We would go so far as to argue that to do so could perpetuate cycles of inequality. However, we should encourage ways of talking and offer means of support for children and young people to process the circumstances they find themselves in.

The links between poverty and mental health are strongly evidenced. For example, an NHS survey in 2017 revealed that children in the lowest income quintile were twice as likely to be diagnosed with an emotional disorder as those in the highest earning quintile.[7] Furthermore, in 2021 Dr Dubicka, Chair of the Child and Adolescent Faculty at the Royal College of Psychiatrists, said, *'poverty is a huge driver of mental health problems, probably the biggest, driver.'*[8] However we should remember that poor homes can be very loving homes, where a number of protective factors are in place. Furthermore, those who come from more affluent homes are by no means immune to mental ill health. In short, we need to be careful not to make assumptions surrounding this, while also being aware of the research.

Being part of a marginalised group is another risk factor for poor mental health. Schools have a duty under the Equality Act 2010[9] to treat people fairly. They must guard against discrimination because of:

1. Race
2. Disability
3. Religion or belief
4. Sex
5. Sexual orientation
6. Gender reassignment
7. Marriage and civil partnership
8. Pregnancy or maternity

Discrimination will impact young people in different ways depending on their level of support and their confidence to ask for help. Also, factors that we are just starting to understand about the brain, such as an individual's level of neuroplasticity, may contribute, but the science has a long way to go in this field before it will benefit people's lived experience. More and more research highlights associations between discrimination—whether an acute attack or more chronic microaggressions—and post-traumatic stress disorder (PTSD).[10] One person may suffer from the symptoms of PTSD, whereas another person's brain may process the experiences differently. What we know is that children or young people who experience discrimination may feel powerless and frustrated, be at a higher risk of being bullied, and struggle to reach their full potential. Certain areas of discrimination, such as racism, will also have the weight of centuries of generational inequality and injustice behind it.

When it comes to mental illness and physical health inequalities, we now know that the relationship is bidirectional. Young adults with serious mental illness are five times more likely to have three or more physical health conditions than those without.[11] Furthermore, it is not just the physical conditions that can affect their life expectancy. Sadly, people with mental illness are over three times more likely to die prematurely in England, and recent studies suggest that this issue is worsening.[12] As the relationship between physical and mental health is two-way, the positive news is that increased levels of good mental health relates to improved physical health and vice versa.

Depending on your school's intake, a lack of extended family ties can also be a considerable challenge in some schools. For example, if a school community has asylum seekers or refugees, these children may be grieving the loss of family ties, which can put a huge pressure on their wellbeing and that of their family. Dr Gabor Maté tells a story of being born in Nazi-occupied Hungary. When his worried mother called the doctor about her son's incessant crying, she was told that all the Jewish babies in his care were crying constantly. As babies, they had no cognitive understanding of what was happening, but could sense the deep sadness of their caregivers.[13] Familial trauma that passes through generations is something all schools will face, but its invisible nature means it won't be easily spotted. Hopefully, with more knowledge and through identifying children and young people at risk of this generational trauma, schools can respond to these needs more effectively. It is, therefore, crucial that the SMHL is aware of the indicators in children within their school whose families may have suffered upheaval or suffering.

Another group often affected by a lack of extended family ties is children who have been taken into care. Obviously, the child would have been separated from their immediate family, but their removal might also affect their ability to regularly contact and visit other relatives. Putting their family ties aside, children in the care system are more likely to have poor mental health because of their experiences before and during care. Studies have revealed that 45% of looked-after children have a diagnosable mental health illness, and up to 80% have recognisable mental health concerns.[14] These figures are deeply worrying, but also unsurprising when we consider that children are taken into care to protect them from abuse or neglect, which they often would have already experienced. Compounding this is the instability of their new life where they are potentially moved between different foster families or homes. In the role of alloparents (those who provide any sort of care to young people who are not their own children) school staff often provide some needed stability and routine to such children's lives.

Lastly, in the past few years, it has become increasingly clear that the impact of the Covid-19 pandemic on people's mental health has not been equal. According to studies, certain groups have been more impacted. These include unemployed people, people with long-term physical or mental health conditions, women, people from ethnic communities,

LGBTQIA+ people and older people who are isolated. We also know that young people have been more affected as they have missed out on education and employment, impacting their mental wellbeing. Those who are already marginalised have often experienced more significant stress and uncertainty, compounding this effect.

How can we gain insight into our intake?

On a practical level, we can do this in several ways. The first is to review the data of the school intake. A valuable tool can be found on the Office for National Statistics website, which explores local income deprivation (the link for this is in the bibliography).[15] It will show you a map of the deprivation data in the area surrounding your school.

This powerful visual tool can be combined with figures such as the pupil premium data in your school. Together, they can be shared with staff along with information on the connection between disadvantage and mental health. Making staff aware of risk factors and having a clear referral process is central to the proactive part of the early identification of pupils with mental health challenges. In some cases, this may also negate the need for later clinical support.

Such data will provide an overview but shouldn't be where developing our insight ends. We also need the voices of the students and parents to give it context, shading, and texture—and they deserve to be heard. Although it is essential to begin with a broad view to assess the background of our pupils, we must remember that ultimately the children we educate come from different worlds, and we must take this into account when we deal with them individually.

As Professor Katherine Weare said in 2016, after conducting a systematic review of whole school best practices worldwide for the Partnership for Wellbeing and Mental Health in Schools, *'The emphasis is on developing a school and classroom climate which builds a sense of connectedness and purpose so that all children can thrive. It also highlights the need to promote staff well-being and particularly to address their stress levels. The findings identify the triggers that can lead to mental health issues such as: lack of trust; com-*

munication and relationship breakdowns; and the possible lack of extended family ties.'[16] From this research came a list of best practice recommendations, one of which was to engage the whole community by promoting pupil voice and peer learning and involve parents, carers, and families.

Therefore, to really protect mental health and wellbeing, schools must build a climate of connectedness and purpose. This means between the school and individual families, but also a connectedness between pupils from different backgrounds. If a lack of trust can be a trigger for mental health issues, one of the aims should be to increase the trust between the school, pupils, and families, which is often reduced in deprived areas due to the day-to-day challenges people face, or parents' own negative experiences of school. One of the first steps towards gaining someone's trust is communication. For this to happen, it cannot be a one-way conversation from the schools to the families; there must be ways for parents and carers to express their views in a format that makes them feel comfortable and heard.

We also know that a child's social, emotional, cognitive, and academic development is strengthened when educators and families have a close working relationship.[17] When the child sees this trust, they are encouraged by the fact that both the school and their family want what is best for them. This collaborative foundation can be created in several ways and, as we see regularly, schools often work hard to foster these positive relationships through initiatives such as tea and toast mornings, parents offering lunch groups or activities for pupils, or after school parent and child cooking courses.

Finally, the SMHL can also consider the local transformation plan, whether there are gaps in provision, and if so, how they can be addressed. In return, the SMHL should have input into the local transformation plan after assessing the earlier points. The local transformation plan is important because it sets out how local services invest in protecting children and young people's mental health. The SMHL will have valuable contributions to add to it about the challenges that local people face regarding their health and mental health. Also, as a SMHL, you will have a unique insight into the challenges young people in your school's area face, which are often not conveyed to anyone at local council level by other sources. So the key is for a SMHL to find out how to have their voices heard in the development and/or reviews of these plans, whether through contacting their local council or the local authority. Some have a named key point of contact, and others are put together more broadly, but it is worth checking for contact details to see how the local education sector is represented. This will ensure that the specific needs of the SMHL's community are given a voice and are included in this important document. This reflects our firm belief that schools should be at the heart of communities.

The school culture

A school culture can be defined by shared beliefs and values on both a conscious and subconscious level. It also incorporates relationships between all members of the community. In the education world there is currently a lively debate about how culture is set within a school. Does it come from the local environment? Or the pupils and their attitudes? How about the staff? Or does it come solely from the leadership team? Ultimately, we return to the age-old question: does a culture come from the top down or the bottom up?

We both enjoy a lively debate, but rather than spending pages outlining our nuanced view, we will mention it briefly. In our opinion, the school culture possesses a collective character shaped by all these influences. Firstly, a leadership team shouldn't, and arguably cannot, impose a culture on a school. Secondly, a leadership team can state what the school culture is, but it doesn't necessarily mean that it's true—just because we repeatedly announce we are filming a documentary called *Islands in the Stream*, doesn't alter the fact that we are, in reality, writing a book. Thirdly, the true school culture, formed by the individuals at the grassroots, can be shaped by the leadership team but only if they are respected. Finally, the school culture also has ghosts of cultures past and ghosts of cultures future (apologies, Mr Dickens). A school leadership team might decide to wipe the slate clean and impose a new culture, but the people living within it will still remember the previous one. Alternatively, they might hear about an impending culture change, and their expectations will outweigh the reality of what can feasibly be delivered.

One concern about imposing a top-down culture from leadership is the risk of imposing middle-class values on pupils who don't share them. So, instead, it's about recognising the culture children are coming from, knowing your school vision, mission, and ethos, and then blending them in a way that respects the diversity within the school. Because ultimately, even though the school is a microcosm with its own expectations and culture, we do not expect the children and young people to leave their own culture at the door. Instead, we want them to take what they learn from a positive and empowering school home with them, and even to radiate it into the wider community.

So, how do we assess our *true* school culture? To do this, we should start with the school vision and mission statement and then consider how this translates into practice in the school. How evident is this in the day-to-day life of the school? For example, the school might say they 'foster a calm environment to encourage learning', but when you walk through the corridors are the children climbing the walls and late for lessons? This doesn't mean the school's vision and mission statement shouldn't be aspirational, but we need to view these factors realistically as there may be an accidental culture in place that negates them.

This is important because if there is a discrepancy between how the leadership and pupils view the school culture, it may lead to a lack of trust. This brings us back to how a lack of trust negatively impacts mental health. It means there is less room for psychological safety, which is the belief you won't be punished for admitting fault or speaking up, and that making mistakes is okay. Also, if we feel safe enough to speak up, we can get proper support quicker and make more progress towards good mental health. Therefore, if a school is asserting a commitment to a mission and a vision that clearly isn't the reality of the situation, you are operating in a bubble of denial. As SMHL you should consider what, if anything, needs changing to develop a sense of psychological safety. Because that sense of security, being cared for, connectedness, and purpose all support mental health.

Using the school's mission statement and vision as a starting point, the leadership could devise statements they believe to be true about the school culture. For example, 'all children feel cared for' or 'people feel safe to make mistakes and learn from them'. These can then be used to engage stakeholders and give pupils and parents a voice in the school culture. A quick way to do this would be to send the statements out as part of a survey, and pupils and parents select to what extent they agree with each statement. However, we prefer using focus groups to gather this information as it allows the SMHL to hear the student voice and listen to the challenges young people face in a particular context. Having a conversation in a relaxed setting that pupils and parents feel comfortable with can open communication channels and establish a meaningful dialogue.

The findings from these types of exercises—whether gathered through a survey or a focus group—can highlight differences in perceptions of school culture. Any dissonance in these perceptions can then be addressed. If parents perceive the school to be a place where children will be judged harshly for making mistakes, for example, what actions can you take to address this—and crucially, how can you communicate them? In this instance, you might decide to introduce a weekly postcard home to celebrate improvements in effort or behaviour. However, it is equally important to emphasise to parents that the purpose of these postcards is to reinforce the school's belief that we can all learn from our mistakes and improve.

Wellbeing Charter

To continue using the information you have gathered in a way that protects mental health and promotes mental wellbeing, consider preparing a wellbeing charter. This can be created collaboratively with pupils and even their families, thereby opening the lines of communication if they need cultivating.

Involving pupils with this is an exciting opportunity, as it is our aim that this charter radiates out into the community. Children have an exceptional ability to challenge entrenched views in a way that an adult advocate might not. Often, a child's perspective breaks down barriers as they have not accumulated the years of bias most adults have. Young people often reach the truth of a matter in a few simple words, while the rest of us tie ourselves up in semantic knots.

Below is our example of what this charter might include. You are welcome to use or adapt it, but even better if yours reflects your unique school setting and voices:

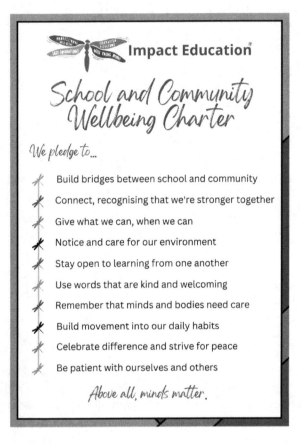

Impact Education

School and Community Wellbeing Charter

We pledge to...

- Build bridges between school and community
- Connect, recognising that we're stronger together
- Give what we can, when we can
- Notice and care for our environment
- Stay open to learning from one another
- Use words that are kind and welcoming
- Remember that minds and bodies need care
- Build movement into our daily habits
- Celebrate difference and strive for peace
- Be patient with ourselves and others

Above all, minds matter.

Before we look at the academic year in the next chapter, take time to consider the following questions in relation to your unique school setting:

1. How does my school's mission statement or values connect with our vision for mental health?
2. What evidence is there for the school's mission statement and values being implemented?
3. What would a good mental health culture look like in my school?

Summary

- Your school environment will be influenced by society and the school culture.

- Being aware of these helps with the proactive promotion of good mental health and prevention of poor mental health.

- Some factors that impact mental health are disadvantage, discrimination, physical ill health, lack of family ties, and contact with the justice system or social services.

- It is useful to gather pupil and parent perceptions of the school culture and address discrepancies between these views and the views of school leadership. Gaps in perceptions of school culture can impact trust, and in turn, trust impacts mental health.

- A wellbeing charter can provide pupils with a voice that can then be radiated into the community.

Chapter Three: The Current

'Even during the summer holidays, it's easy to recall how quickly the pace of the school day can crank up again and how important it is for all staff to have strategies to face this.'
– J.F. (SMHL, Somerset)

Now that we understand the society that feeds into our school environment and the impact of the school culture, there is one other factor we must consider—the academic year, or as we like to view it, the current.

The movement of the stream, what drives it forward, is the passing of the school year. Most people who work in schools will confirm that there is a reassuring predictability to its flow; it is cyclical in nature. Like all currents, there will be times when it is more turbulent, when different challenges will arise throughout the year. Covid-19 was a huge boulder dropped into the stream, forcing the current down either side and increasing the pressure. The pressure still hasn't returned to 'normal' and the reactiveness of the DfE, and frequent turnover of education secretaries, add to it. In these circumstances, anticipating the pressures that can be predicted and prepared for can prevent a potential maelstrom.

The academic year for school staff

The previous two chapters leaned more towards protecting and promoting the pupils' mental health and wellbeing, but it is equally essential to do the same for the school's staff. When it comes to the current, it is the staff who are more at risk from its impact as part of their role is to steer the pupils through the academic year. As we know, being an educator is not an easy job. There is often a heavy workload combined with a great deal of responsibility, and many will be suffering from fatigue towards the end of a school term.

From our own experience as teachers, most staff are more relaxed at the beginning of the academic year, after the summer break. There is a palpable air of anticipation as people gear up to meet their new classes or take on new roles. It is a fresh start, and most are ready to tackle it, believing that with the right preparation the year will run smoothly.

We remember that at the beginning of September, we felt as though we were teetering at the top of a slope, anticipating what lay ahead and preparing to race down to it. The school doors would open, and we would set off, picking up the pace along the way. We would deliver back-to-back lessons while dealing with issues arising from students who were struggling and their parents. If your role is part of the Senior Leadership Team (SLT), you will include colleagues in that list as well. As the days turn into weeks, the number of situations needing our attention multiply. Maybe an intervention to support a struggling pupil didn't have the desired outcome, so we return to the student or parent and devise a new plan of action, but in the meantime, there are still more pupils and parents turning to us that need our help. We would also be supporting children who are under-achieving, absent, or disaffected, or perhaps disruptive in class. And then, as we are being pulled in a multitude of directions, it is time for the pupils to be assessed. We limp into the October half-term exhausted, and with a pile of assessment papers to mark.

From our experience of working in comprehensive schools, the week or two before the October half-term are particularly fraught, and we could trace that pressure throughout the school year in-line with assessment periods. It lifts again around May half-term, and we would begin to feel that the end is in sight. But each school is unique—as we understand from listening to our colleagues in primary schools, the build-up to the annual nativity could fell even the hardiest of teaching staff.

Therefore, as SMHL, it would be useful to chart the pressure points for the staff in your school. You could do this from your own experience, observations, or even survey colleagues. Another way to gather information is to review staff absence for the past few years and see if patterns emerge. This helps because a percentage of these absences will be for mental health, not just physical health. In fact, the data suggests more absences are for mental health.[18] This auditing of pressure points will allow you to plan mental health provisions for the school year (more on this in Chapters 6, 7 and 8). Staff won't then have to rely on informal support from colleagues, which often melts away when there are heightened stress levels across the board.

These pressure points are also when a SMHL might feel overwhelmed as more and more staff members turn to them and try to hand over the work or situations that are impacting their mental health. It's important to remember, particularly if you are a very giving person, that your role as SMHL is not to take on everyone else's workload to ease their strain. Instead, it is to *oversee* the implementation of provisions to aid mental health and wellbeing. There must be boundaries in place to protect your own mental health, and from our experience of working with hundreds of SMHLs, this is what many struggle with. Instead of taking on what is affecting their mental health, you can steer them towards the systems, procedures, and practices you have already implemented, which we will cover in Part 2.

Another challenge you will face, related to the school year, is *when* to share your findings and procedures regarding promoting good mental health. Staff engagement with these systems is vital as they must be alert to the signs and symptoms of mental health needs in pupils and know what procedures to follow when concerns are raised. One of the most pressing challenges in any school or college context is finding the time for staff to engage. Because of the focus on academic achievement and teaching commitments, staff often do not have the capacity to review or share resources that could support mental health. This challenge of information sharing should first be addressed by the SMHL choosing a less pressurised time to share their findings with the teaching staff (for example, at the start of the academic year) and ensuring that procedures are clear and easily accessible.

The academic year for pupils

When it comes to the pupils' experience of the academic year, we must remember that they have different pressure points to staff, although some may overlap, such as around assessments.

A key point is that for most staff (not all, sadly), the holidays will usually be a time when they have some freedom and autonomy over what they do. But for some children, they are totally at the mercy of the circumstances surrounding their home life. If a child lives in a household where they witness domestic violence, for example, their holidays will obviously not be a time of carefree relaxation. In fact, the behaviour of a child who lives in these awful circumstances will likely deteriorate as they approach the holiday period because they are so worried about being at home the entire time. Socio-economic pressures can also exacerbate domestic tensions meaning that school holidays create an increasing financial strain on some families, and children and young people often feel this stress.

We should consider the pressure points for suicide as well. *The Millennium Cohort Study* published in November 2020 by UCL stated that of the 19,000 seventeen-year-olds surveyed, 7% confirmed that they had attempted suicide.[19] Obvious pressure points are around periods of assessments or exams. In *Suicide by Children and Young People* published in 2017 by Manchester University, it is stated, *'Suicide in students under 20 occurred more often in April and May, conventionally exam months. Only 12% were reported to be seeing student counselling services.'*[20]

As SMHL, it would be helpful to chart these pressure points for pupils too, ideally in a collaborative way with pupils and parents. As well as looking at attendance records, you could also review behaviour records to see if there are times in the year when behaviour is particularly challenging and may signal a cry for help from some pupils. Both are signs of pressure points that can be predicted and prepared for.

The flow of the academic year

To help with the proactive part of the SMHL role, consider the nuances of your own school year so that you can prepare well thought out solutions. This will aid mental health within the school environment by showing an awareness and understanding of the pressures, and will also assist with the reactive part of your role when it is required as you will have already considered potential situations that may arise.

Below, we have suggested insights into the academic year in a typical school in relation to staff. The table is by no means an exhaustive list, but the practice of reflecting on the pressures on staff at particular points can help you alert school leadership to think about ways of mitigating these pressures. As SMHL, you can't fix all things or make them disappear, but you can consider ways to ease the load.

General pressures throughout the year for teachers:

- Poor behaviour
- Low-level disruption in lessons
- Parental pressures
- Ofsted
- Learning walks
- Book checks

Leadership actions to mitigate these general pressures:

- Ensure a robust behaviour policy—a whole-school approach to managing behaviour
- Foster positive relationships with parents, offering clear and regular communication through newsletters or email updates
- Distribute a clear timetable for book checks and learning walks at the start of the year, and provide staff with the criteria/rationale for these decisions
- Ensure book checks and learning walks are scheduled around other pressure points on the school calendar

Term 1 – Pressures specific to the term

- Establishing new relationships
- Learning a new timetable
- Establishing expectations
- Assessing the learning needs of the new class/es
- Tiredness—the longest term!
- Physical illness
- Ensuring pupils who have been absent due to illness catch up
- Assessments and marking
- Keeping children motivated through a long term with dark mornings and poor weather
- Parents' evenings
- Open evenings/information evenings

Leadership actions to mitigate them

- Phased return of year groups
- Establish expectations as a whole school, to be reinforced in classrooms
- Shared banks of resources collated centrally for pupils who are absent/need to catch up with missed work
- Allow staff directed time for collaborative planning

- Acknowledge the challenges of the term and create spaces for staff to connect, e.g. a shared breakfast before school or social activities at the end of the school day

- Ensure additional pressures such as learning walks and book checks do not coincide with late evenings in school for staff

- Have strong leadership presence in all areas of the school at parents' evenings and after school events

- Thank staff in person, regularly and genuinely

- Take opportunities to share the impact of the work staff perform, including both staff and parents, giving examples and success stories

Term 2 – Pressures specific to the term

- January dip in mood

- Physical illness

- Assessment points/mock exams

- Additional marking load from assessments and/or regular exam practice

- Additional intervention/support classes as pupils approach SATs/GCSEs/A levels

- Demands of ensuring curriculum is covered and revised

- Providing emotional support and reassurance for pupils and/or parents

- Moderation

Leadership actions to mitigate them

- Support marking of assessments by prioritising whole class feedback

- Ensure curriculum coverage is planned

- Allow directed time for collaborative planning

- Share the marking load for mock exams fairly among staff

✳   If possible, when certain departments are going to carry a particularly heavy marking load, budget for cover staff or allow TA to supervise silent assessments while teaching staff mark

✳   Use intervention and support classes judiciously and have this planned with staffing, to be published as early in the year as possible—be proactive rather than reactive around this

✳   Create a central support hub for students and/or parents—a key point of contact they can call on or a room they can go to if needed

✳   Meet with curriculum leads early in the year to establish the time they will need for moderation and other assessment requirements. Plan this into the directed time allocation well in advance

✳   Ensure staff that put in additional hours for extra sessions, student support or a particularly heavy marking load are recognised and rewarded appropriately—whether that be a card or note, or time in lieu

Term 3 – Pressures specific to the term

- Preparing for transition

- Report writing

- End of year assessment marking

- Reviewing class lists and needs for the next academic year

- Planning and preparation of curriculum and resourcing for the next academic year

Leadership actions to mitigate them

- Streamline assessment points and the report writing process for staff

- Ensure each year group or department are allotted appropriate time for reviewing new class lists and planning the curriculum and resources for the next academic year

- Celebrate achievements—verbally, in writing, as a whole staff and by individually thanking staff for specific aspects of their work

- Give staff examples of how their work has made a difference

The following year, you can review the previous year's plan and evaluate what worked for the school by asking questions such as, what was most effective for the pupils? Which interventions should we do more or less to help staff? This will build in the process of monitoring and assessing, which is vital to improving the school's approach to mental health and wellbeing.

To begin assessing the flow of your own school's academic year, and before we dive into the second part of the book, take time for reflection and consider the following questions:

1. What pressure points have I noticed from a personal point of view throughout the academic year?
2. When have I noticed my colleagues becoming particularly stressed or overwhelmed?
3. What are the pressure points for the students in my school setting?
4. When would be the best time of year to share my findings and procedures for aiding good mental health?
5. What format or method of distribution is easiest for staff to engage with?

Summary

⚹   Certain points during the academic year will be more pressurised for staff and pupils.

⚹   These points of pressure can have an adverse effect on mental wellbeing.

⚹   Because they are often predictable, they can be prepared for and their impact reduced.

⚹   To assess your own school year, consider speaking to colleagues and pupils about when they feel these pressure points. You can also review attendance and behaviour records.

⚹   Consider preparing a table charting your school year and the interventions the senior leadership could make to reduce their potential effect on mental wellbeing.

Part Two:
Beneath the Surface

Chapter Four: The Value of Schools

'The more reading I do, the more I like the preventative approach and can see how we do so much already in school.'
– D.H. (SMHL, Bristol)

When we are told about upcoming changes in education, we may feel this casts an unfavourable light on what is already in place. We can feel despondent about a lack of recognition and may focus on what is *not* being done rather than celebrating and expanding on what is already in place.

The last few chapters will have hopefully highlighted the importance of mental wellbeing and mental health provisions in a school context. However, at their core, schools are already infused with conditions that engender good mental health. Learning, creativity, and relationships all aid mental wellbeing and mental health. These three things are at the centre of every school and, therefore, their value cannot be overstated.

But how schools support mental health goes deeper than what we see on the surface. Schools provide children and young people with new adult relationships outside of the family. A particular type of trust will hopefully grow between teachers and pupils. When epistemic trust is in place, pupils will consider the knowledge being imparted to them as beneficial and worth learning. Professor Peter Fonagy, Head of the Division of

Psychology and Language Sciences at UCL, once said, *'Our epistemic superhighway, our "knowledge superhighway", is open when we feel that someone is interested in us as a person.'*[21] This openness to learning flourishes through trust. Schools, by definition, can access this beneficial kind of learning because if strong relationships arise between the students and staff, the pupils have a biological propensity to learn more than they would from other sources perceived as less trustworthy.

As well as the educator and student relationships, the ones between staff members are also important. Teachers will likely have a few close friends among their colleagues, and children can observe healthy, mutually beneficial friendships. This role modelling can demonstrate what true friendships look like and aid students' understanding of how these meaningful relationships nourish our health and wellbeing.

As well as promoting mental wellbeing, schools also shield pupils from poor mental health by providing a sanctuary, access to a meal each day and a sense of consistency. At their best, schools can stem the tide of the outside world. Children can go to school, speak to trusted adults and rely on the steady routines to anchor them, because routines aid us when other parts of our lives are chaotic and unsettled. Nothing has highlighted these points more than the impact of school closures during the Covid-19 pandemic. In the most extreme cases, schools save lives, which is why a mental health policy should complement the essential work of safeguarding.

Ultimately, there is a reason schools have been tasked with promoting good mental health—they have an innate ability to nurture children and effect change.

The mental health policy and provisions

When you first take on the role of SMHL, it might feel slightly overwhelming, particularly if there isn't a mental health policy already in place in your school. However, you are not alone in this reaction as we hear of it time and again from other SMHLs who we train:

I have just taken on the role of the SMHL and, although excited, I'm also fairly nervous about the workload. It feels like a huge responsibility, and there's a lot to learn and consider when I am already pressed for time. It would be much easier to get to grips with if there weren't so many interruptions. As the DSL, there are times when I have to drop everything else to focus on a safeguarding incident. This has to, and always will come first. The SMHL role would be more manageable if I could share the responsibility with someone else, but the funding is for one person, and that person is me.

There are several initiatives that link into mental health already happening across the school, but I'm not in charge of them. I worry about whether I have the authority to link them up. Because I didn't initiate them, I'm not sure if I can just step in and try to lead them. Will I be treading on other people's toes? Thinking about this now, there are other members of staff who I should meet up with and perhaps ask if they will come on board as part of the team to drive things forward. I just don't know when I'm going to find the time to meet with them.

If I'm honest, there is a lot I don't know about in terms of what is available in the local community. I want to do the best for my pupils, this is why I became a teacher, but I worry there might not be enough support beyond the school walls and that my workload will just increase because of this.

This is what Part Two of the book will focus on—the practical guidance a SMHL needs, how to adapt this to their school, the tools of implementation, and information on how to make the role manageable.

When approaching or reviewing the role first assess whether there is already a mental health policy. If there is, it would be a good idea to review it and check what it contains as it may require revising or expanding. If there isn't a mental health policy, you should consider whether to create one. At present, there is no regulatory requirement to have one, but a well-thought-out mental health policy will help make your procedures clear and accessible to the school's staff. The creation of the policy itself could even benefit mental health and wellbeing within your school as it provides an extra level of focus on the subject. When the DfE carried out its review of mental health procedures in schools between 2016 and 2018, it found a mixture of approaches. Some schools had a separate mental health policy, and others simply referenced mental health through other policies. You can approach it either way, but the DfE concluded that schools with a separate mental health policy offered a wider range of provisions to support the mental health of *all* pupils, not just the ones with diagnosed mental health conditions and needs.[22]

It is a substantial undertaking to create a mental health policy, or even to revise an existing one in a meaningful way, and one a SMHL cannot do alone. It will need to be done in conjunction with others in the school's senior leadership, such as the head teacher, DSL, Special Educational Needs and Disabilities Coordinator (SENDCo) and the person in charge of health and safety. Working with other people can introduce new challenges, so it may be useful to consider how you will approach this (there is more about leadership in the next chapter). For the moment, these colleagues could be eased into the process if the SMHL can be clear on what the policy should contain. Below is our suggestion:

A mental health policy should consider including...

1. A policy statement encompassing:

    ✳ Definitions of mental health, mental wellbeing, and mental illness

    ✳ A statement of your commitments to mental health and mental wellbeing and the policy's aim.

2. Key staff members:

   🪰 Who is the SMHL

   🪰 Who is the supporting team

3. The whole-school approach:

   🪰 What the approach includes (such as 'training for staff, pupils and parents')

4. Systems and procedures:

   🪰 Who can raise a concern

   🪰 The procedure to follow if a concern is raised about a pupil

   🪰 The procedure to follow if a concern is raised about a member of staff

5. Support and signposting offered at the school for pupils and staff:

   🪰 Internal available resources such as social skills groups, the school nurse, ELSAs or first aiders for mental health etc.

   🪰 External available resources such as GPs, CYPMHS self-referral, Young Minds or Education Support etc.

6. Identifying warning signs:

   🪰 What behaviours and physical changes staff will be trained to recognise

   🪰 What issues staff will be trained to recognise

Whether there is a mental health policy or not, it is important to consider other policies the school has in place, as they may overlap with the mental health policy and can either be referenced within it or provide a basis for its content. These policies should complement one another, include a cohesive approach, and reference each other. If this is not the case, or if the procedures clash, this may need to be brought to the attention of the SLT.

Most importantly, we should also consider the school's *practices* regarding these policies. This brings us back to the school culture: the policies need to be lived not just laminated. If there is a discrepancy between what the policies contain and what happens in practice, this may impact trust. Policies and procedures you should consider are:

- Safeguarding
- Special educational needs
- Bullying
- Behaviour
- Equality and diversity
- Teacher appraisal and capability
- Staff sickness and absence

The school improvement plan (SIP) should also be considered alongside the above. As the SIP deals with the key areas of improvement the school needs to focus on and the targets that support this focus, it might be a document the SMHL wants to review to check that mental health is being appropriately represented.

Something else that can be considered in relation to mental health is the school mission statement. It may be helpful for you to review this statement and consider how to link the school's core values to your vision for mental health.

Once the policies and procedures are addressed, we can look at the school's approach to mental health and wellbeing from another angle. We always want students and staff to have a voice, so we should speak to them about what they value in the school. There might be protective factors about which we are unaware that are important for mental health and wellbeing. If they haven't been referenced in the mental health policy, they might deserve mentioning to help protect their longevity. One lovely example of this we heard about recently was from a school with a 'meet and greet' policy. Every morning, a teacher stands at the gate to greet students as they enter. It might be a small thing in our eyes, but to the students, when asked, it made them feel welcome and that someone is pleased to see them. Another example is of staff sharing what they are reading on their email signature or on their classroom door. It makes them human and approachable; it might even start a new conversation between two bookworms rather than 'educator and student'. A small thing, yes, but still worth protecting if it contributes to building trust and fostering relationships between educators and students.

Other protective factors might not have been raised by staff and students, either because they are unaware of them or do not directly link them to mental health. For example, if you are working within a multi-academy trust, what is on offer within the trust that children and staff could access? This might include the extra-curricular activities in place. A simple, targeted pre- and post-questionnaire could establish whether the activity explicitly or implicitly supports mental health. Perhaps you could visit the clubs to see for yourself whether they have facilities or routines that aid mental health, such as providing students with a quiet space, potentially reducing stress levels.

If you want to formalise this process into a more structured audit, we recommend reviewing the school's provisions based on the following eight principles taken from *Promoting Children and Young People's Mental Health and Wellbeing: A Whole School or College Approach* produced by Public Health England and the DfE in 2015:[23]

1. **Leadership and management** *that supports and champions efforts to promote emotional health and wellbeing*
2. *An* **ethos and environment** *that promotes respect and values diversity*
3. **Curriculum teaching and learning** *to promote resilience and support social and emotional learning*
4. *Enabling* **student voice** *to influence decisions*

5. **Staff development** *to support their own wellbeing and that of students*
6. **Identifying need and monitoring impact** *of interventions*
7. **Working with Parents and carers**
8. **Targeted support** *and appropriate referral*

If you would like a more in-depth audit but don't feel that you have the time or experience to do this, there are organisations, including ourselves, who provide an external audit of the school's approach to mental health and wellbeing. An external audit can provide an objective viewpoint and help the SMHL and SLT recognise the gaps in their policies.

To begin considering your school's approach to mental health and mental wellbeing, you can review the following questions and rank them as either red, amber, or green. The results will then highlight areas that need to be addressed.

How well does your setting...

1. Communicate their commitment to mental health and wellbeing to the whole school community?
2. Ensure pupils know who they can talk to both in and out of school?
3. Create quiet areas for pupils to regulate their emotions?
4. Communicate vision, values, and high expectations clearly and consistently?
5. Recognise and challenge stigma around mental ill health?
6. Reinforce positive values visually, e.g. through displays?
7. Support students to map out a sense of their future, including aspirations, hopes, and purpose, which are meaningful to each individual?
8. Celebrate the efforts and achievements of staff and students regularly?
9. Ensure information for pupils, staff, and parents is clear and accessible via the website, leaflets etc., especially out-of-hours

helplines and websites?
10. Encourage pupils and staff to express their identity (sexuality, cultural experiences etc.)?
11. Promote equality and diversity and challenge discrimination?
12. Provide a strong and effective anti-bullying programme?
13. Create opportunities to develop roles and responsibilities?

Summary

✱   The value of schools stretches way beyond the academic arena.

✱   Schools already have many policies and procedures to support mental health and mental wellbeing, and these should be consistent in their approach and reference each other. These policies include safeguarding, equality and diversity, special educational needs, bullying and behaviour, teacher appraisal and capability, and staff sickness and absence.

✱   The SMHL may choose to create a mental health policy if there is not one already in place. A mental health policy is not compulsory but can aid the range of provisions available to assist pupils with their mental health.

✱   An internal or external audit of the whole-school approach to mental health and mental wellbeing can highlight areas that need to be addressed.

Chapter Five: How to Lead (and where to begin)

*'I really need to bring all staff along with me, so I need to create
a way to ensure they have ownership of the changes.'*
– N.O. (SMHL, Sussex)

To make the SMHL role impactful and manageable, you need a whole-school approach, preferably with a supportive team to work alongside you. Whether you have a ten-person line-up or approach the role alone, you will still require leadership skills to effect change and deliver the best approach to mental health that is within your power.

We understand some of you will be head teachers or members of the SLT who would have previously studied leadership theory, but alongside these experienced leaders and managers, many SMHLs will be entering their first leadership role. In the case of someone new to leadership, it is particularly important to have a grounding in its theory as you will often have to guide senior teaching staff and more experienced senior leaders.

A leadership approach encompasses more than just your colleagues. It will also include parents, carers and pupils. It will therefore be part of your role to persuade a large group of people with different backgrounds, experiences, and objectives to embrace your approach to mental health. Start by communicating your plans to pupils, parents and staff in a way that makes them receptive. After all, this is the core of leadership. It is about communicating a vision so that it becomes a shared one, then bringing a community along with you to an end goal.

Leadership styles

Whole libraries could be filled with books about leadership styles (slightly niche libraries, we admit), and it is beyond the remit of this book to cover the hundreds of leadership methods in existence. Instead, we will focus on three popular styles of leadership SMHLs tend to adopt: servant, transformational and authentic.

Servant Leader

The concept of servant leadership is largely attributed to Robert Greenleaf, who published *Servant Leadership: A Journey into the Nature of Power and Greatness* in 1977. His book remains in print and is viewed as a leadership classic. His theories have their roots in many religious doctrines, with some critics arguing that Jesus Christ is the actual founder of servant leadership, not Greenleaf.

A servant leader believes that their role is to serve those around them. This will extend to putting those needs above their own. They will focus on team members as individuals rather than the organisation as a whole. There is a focus on growth for these individuals, including their health as well as their professional needs. The theory behind this approach is that when the needs of the individual are met and their talents nurtured, the whole organisation benefits.

Servant leadership is a move away from a more mainstream leadership viewpoint that the needs of a company or organisation are paramount.

To lead in this manner as a SMHL, you could consider the following actions:

✳ Consider the needs of each individual's mental health, regardless of their position in the hierarchy of the school.

✳ Listen to their contributions and concerns and encourage a diversity of opinion.

✳ Prioritise a culture of trust.

✳ Care about the needs of the individuals like they are your own.

✳ Encourage those below you to embrace roles of responsibility when it comes to implementing mental health provisions.

Max is a kind and compassionate leader who recognises that each member of staff is doing their best. During the most recent 'subject focus' week, he was carrying out paired observations of staff as part of the school's quality assurance procedures for teaching and learning. One of the teachers observed was clearly very stressed and feeling the pressure of being watched. There was a sense during the lesson that she knew it wasn't going as well as she wanted, which only seemed to heighten her stress levels and negatively impacted on the lesson even further.

Following the lesson, he sat down with the other member of the SLT who had observed the lesson with him. They were meeting to discuss the feedback that should be given to the member of staff. Max strongly felt that the lesson clearly wasn't representative of the staff member's typical teaching and that the feedback should reflect this.

> He also felt that the staff member should be given the chance to be observed again if they wished, for the sake of their wellbeing. The other member of the SLT argued that it was important to follow the same procedure for all observations and give feedback in the same way for everyone, but Max remained adamant that staff should be dealt with on a case-by-case basis and their wellbeing taken into account. His SLT colleague respected Max's decision due to a history of excellent outcomes in terms of coaching and mentoring staff.

Transformational Leader

Transformational leadership was first developed in the second half of the 20th Century by sociologist James V. Downton. Later, leadership expert James Burns published *Leadership* in 1978, where he discusses transformational and transactional leadership. It is still a very popular method of leadership and is epitomised in the style of people like Steve Jobs, Oprah Winfrey, and Jeff Bezos.

A transformational leadership approach requires a leader to inspire a group of people to embrace a shared vision and put aside their immediate self-interests to enact change. It usually requires a strong, charismatic leader who can motivate people to embrace a goal and work together on realising it. In return, the transformational leader will encourage and upskill team members in leadership qualities through coaching and mentoring.

Transformational leadership is characterised by what Bernard M. Bass termed the four 'I's:[24]

- **Idealised influence:** They influence their team by embodying the changes and qualities they want others to embrace. They are a role model who is admired and trusted, and people want to emulate them. In essence, they are charismatic.
- **Inspirational motivation:** They inspire and motivate their

team by creating a vision and, importantly, ensuring that they successfully communicate it. Team members understand the importance and meaning of the vision and consequently share it too.

- **Intellectual stimulation:** They are dynamic leaders who question assumptions and view situations in other lights. They encourage this lateral thinking in their team members and hugely value creativity.

- **Individualized consideration:** They are genuinely concerned about the personal growth of the individuals within their team and address needs on a personal basis through coaching or mentoring where needed. A supportive environment is valued.

To lead in this manner as a SMHL, you could consider the following actions:

- Develop a clear vision for your school's approach to mental health and work on conveying this vision in an inspiring way.

- Select a team to support you who will embrace your vision and make it their own.

- Open up lines of communication regarding mental health with pupils and staff.

- Be prepared to explain your vision on a grand level to a large audience and also to an individual.

- Encourage a supportive environment that fosters trust.

Riley is passionate about ensuring good mental health and wellbeing for all members of the school community. She regularly holds staff briefings that focus on her vision for ensuring that the school raises levels of wellbeing for staff and pupils, and staff are inspired by the changes she wants to make, her ideas and her drive to improve the culture of the school. Some staff are concerned about additional workload and some seem dubious that much will change at all because 'things have always been this way'. However, Riley has created a team of likeminded staff who share her vision and they have gone on to create focus groups of staff, parents and pupils and have created a wellbeing noticeboard.

Although she realises members of her team are taking on extra work to support her vision, Riley can see that they are approaching the goals she's laid out in a creative way and she is there to support them in developing their own leadership skills. She doesn't mind stepping back and taking an overview of the work to improve wellbeing because she trusts her team to get it done, just as they trust in her vision and the long-term goals she has laid out.

Authentic Leader

The theory of authentic leadership began in the 1960s but became a popular model when Bill George published *Authentic Leadership* in 2003. In the last couple of decades, there has been a surge of papers written about it, but it is more open to interpretation than the other two leadership styles.

What is generally agreed is that authentic leaders do not assume a role or persona when they lead. Instead, they are self-aware, true to their own personality and genuine in their belief in what they are doing. They essentially go by the Socratic maxim, 'Know thyself,' and act in an open manner supported by self-reflection. Because they are reliable and clear on their beliefs and values, they foster trust within their team. It is with this investment of trust that they lead. In addition, there is an inherently moral element to authentic leadership in that they endeavour to work in an ethical manner. They act for the benefit of the greater organisation rather than their own self-interest.

When it comes to their relationship with their team, authentic leaders are nurturing individuals who create a positive culture. They invest in their team members' futures by focusing on their strengths and encouraging feedback and diverse opinions.

To lead in this manner as a SMHL, you could consider the following actions:

🪰 Express, through your actions, that you wholeheartedly believe in the benefit of a consistent school-wide approach to improve mental health and mental wellbeing.

🪰 Take time for self-reflection and assessment of what is working in your approach and what requires change.

🪰 Be clear on your beliefs surrounding mental health and the school approach.

🪰 Prioritise nurturing trust in a shared ethos.

🪰 Focus on encouraging feedback and welcome other opinions.

Anil knows that a position of leadership—particularly when leading on something as important as mental health and wellbeing—is a huge responsibility. He takes this seriously and his staff can see the work he puts in to making his vision for a whole school approach to mental health a success. He is always up to date with his reading on the latest research and legislation and is very clear about what is expected of schools. He has thoughtfully considered how all of this might be applied to his own

> school and has prepared staff training, clear goals, an action plan and resources.
>
> He knows that some staff are already feeling stressed and overworked and are therefore resistant to the changes he wants to make. He tries to be mindful of this by planning changes carefully and only introducing fully formed ideas when he can outline the support that will be available and is clear about how the impact on staff will be managed. Because of this, staff trust that he will move the school's mental health culture forward in a sustainable way. He feeds back to staff regularly about the impact of each change made and so they see the benefit of all actions taken.

All three styles have pros and cons, and one might suit you better. We have seen all three styles of leadership work well, but the most common fit for senior mental health leads seems to be the authentic leader. That could be because it revolves around being true to who you are and having a commitment and belief in the cause you are promoting. This approach elevates trust, which, as we now know, is an influencing factor in mental health and mental wellbeing. We might be making a presupposition, but a SMHL will be passionate about improving the school environment for the benefit of others (we are yet to be proven wrong on this), and this leadership style supports that level of integrity.

Identifying your team

Having a supportive team will relieve the pressure of feeling *solely* responsible for promoting good mental health within your school, thereby aiding your own mental wellbeing. It will also help streamline the organisational approach, make roles and responsibilities clear and distinct, and allow a cohesive and targeted preventative approach. Finally, it will provide a sounding board when you face some of the ethical dilemmas we will discuss in the next chapter.

If you are in a small school or operate in a highly specific context, you might find yourself doing many—even all—of these roles yourself. If that is the case, you could establish a support system by contacting staff in similar positions in other local schools.

It is a good idea to consider your team by making a list of who you could invite to join you. The following list is a suggestion of the key personnel you might wish to include (but is not limited to them):

Potential candidates for a mental health team

1. Headteacher/deputy headteacher (with pastoral responsibility)

These are the people who steer the ship, weigh up conflicting priorities and hold the purse strings. You will report the impact of your initiatives to them, and they will designate time for mental health training. They are also the people who you will need approval from for whole-school changes.

2. Special educational needs and disabilities co-ordinator (SENDCo)

Pupils with SEND have more risk factors for poor mental health and so liaising with the SENDCo to discuss interventions and monitoring impact is important.

3. Designated safeguarding lead (DSL)

Likewise, students who have safeguarding concerns are more likely to suffer from poor mental health. An effective working relationship with the DSL (if this is not you) is key to your role. If you occupy both roles, it is important to consider from where you can draw support and supervision.

4. Local authority virtual head

Appointed by the local authority to have an overview of looked-after children, this professional will influence pupil premium funding and have an overview of any external intervention.

5. Personal, social, health and economic education lead (PSHE lead)

A close ally for the SMHL with a responsibility for mental health in the PSHE curriculum.

6. Heads of year/pastoral staff

Staff who will deliver assemblies, design activities for tutor time, and who will often be the first port of call for pupils and parents when issues arise.

7. First aiders for mental health

This is a group that you might consider creating if they are not already in existence at your school. Having a team of first aiders trained to support staff and students signals the school's commitment to mental health, reduces stigma, increases the level of knowledge in the school and provides the first port of call for those who are struggling. Although the Health & Safety Executive has not yet made mental health first aiders mandatory in the way that physical first aiders are, they are recommended as good practice. We recommend a ratio of one mental health first aider to every fifteen members of staff and that no single person be left isolated in this role within a school.

As well as these key staff members who could form part of your team, there are other stakeholders you will need to 'take with you' on your journey and to share your vision:

- Governors will have input into the SIP and take a strategic overview of the school's leadership. It's important that they are aware of and agree with the vision behind the plan for mental health provisions. They should also know how this aligns with the school's values and mission, the benefits of the approach and how you are monitoring the impact of your work and any changes. Supportive governors can help you drive your ethos forward by making it a strategic priority.
- Parents and carers are an important part of the school community. Engaging them will increase pupil trust and promote good mental health as they will know that everyone around them supports their best interests. This also plays an important part in reducing stigma and ensuring that pupils hear consistent messages.
- Pupils' input into mental health provisions has been shown to improve student engagement and, subsequently, the positive outcomes of provision. It also feeds into the trust element by having their voices heard and acknowledged. You may use a route such as a school council or wellbeing ambassadors as a conduit for the views of others but it is important to capture the voices of all pupils as far as possible, so a form to fill in during tutor time or a quick online questionnaire could be another option.
- Classroom and associate staff are essential, because if any change is going to be successful and sustained, you cannot just focus on the leadership team. This means sharing your vision and providing them with knowledge and procedures so that they can confidently embrace the whole-school approach.

Where to begin leading

In the last chapter, we discussed the benefits of having a mental health policy. Whether you decide to have one or use other policies instead, they need to translate into practices and provisions. There must be a whole-school approach, and sharing best practice is one of the most salient places to start. Professor Katherine Weare provided a framework in 2016 after conducting a systematic review of whole-school best practices worldwide[25] (mentioned previously in Chapter 2).

Overall, best practice recommendations that emerged were:

1. Take a whole-school approach and implement it carefully:

   - Start with a positive and universal focus on wellbeing

   - Develop a supportive school and classroom climate and ethos

   - Identify and intervene early

   - Take a long-term approach

   - Promote the wellbeing of staff and tackle staff stress

2. Engage the whole community:

   - Promote pupil voice and peer learning

   - Involve parents, carers, and families

3. Prioritise professional learning and staff development:

   ✳ Understand risk and resilience to actively respond to problems and difficulties

   ✳ Help all staff with predictable change and transitions

4. Implement targeted interventions (including curriculum):

   ✳ Use a range of leaders for specific programmes

   ✳ Teach social and emotional skills

5. Provide clear boundaries and robust policies

6. Connect appropriately with approaches to behaviour management:

   ✳ Understand the causes of behaviour

7. Implement targeted responses and identify specialist pathways:

   ✳ Provide clear pathways of help and referral

   ✳ Provide more intensive input for those with difficulties

This will be the framework you refer to when considering your best practice approach following the auditing work you did in the previous chapter. Moreover, as well as auditing to identify where gaps exist in your policies and procedures, you may also want to consider the following three points as well:

Space, Time, Data

✳ **Space:** What spaces are available in the school for interventions, support sessions or as 'safe places'? Are there spaces that could be used creatively, for example, a corner of the school library?

✳ **Time:** What inset time or directed time is available for whole staff training? What assembly time is available to disseminate knowledge to pupils? How can tutor time be used? When will interventions take place for students identified as needing educational/non-clinical intervention?

✳ **Data:** Where pupils are identified as a concern (whether through staff referrals, discussions with the SENDCo, or meetings with the DSL), how will data on attendance, achievement, attention, and behaviour be collated and used to monitor them and/or evaluate the impact of any interventions? Will this data also be used to monitor the effectiveness of a whole-school preventative approach by tracking the attendance, achievement, attention, and behaviour of certain groups, such as looked-after children (LAC), pupil premium (PP), SEND, etc.?

Once you have the relevant information to formulate a whole-school strategic plan, the next step is to look at the gaps (see Chapter 10 for some common trends and themes) and set meaningful but manageable goals that include a realistic time allocation.

Because we are committing to long-term change, we will need long-term goals that are revisited and revisable. It is also beneficial to include these in the SIP. You might be revisiting the same goal each year for three, four or five years, but with each passing year, it will become more embedded in school culture, and staff will become more expert. For this reason, deciding on just a few key goals that will remain in place for several years can help a new culture become established.

Once you have decided on your long-term goals that will be included in the school improvement plan, it's time to consider how these will be achieved in the mid-term (yearly targets) and the short-term (termly action plans). An example of a long-term goal might be, 'Have a clear system for identifying students needing early intervention and support and monitor the effectiveness of interventions.' This could be broken down into three mid-term targets. For example:

Year 1: Staff are trained in identifying the early signs of poor mental health and are confident about when and how to refer to the SMHL/team in school, who intervene as appropriate.

Year 2: (Year 1 target revisited for consolidation) There are a range of early intervention support options available. Their effectiveness is monitored by tracking the impact on pupil behaviour, punctuality, attendance, and attainment.

Year 3: (Year 1 and 2 targets revisited for consolidation) Students are assigned specific types of early intervention according to individual needs, liaising closely with NHS mental health teams or other external providers to ensure wrap-around support is provided.

This can then be divided into termly action plans, for example, for Year 1:

Term 1: Initial staff training about mental health, staff roles (what is expected and what is not), and how to identify the signs of poor mental health. A referral system is introduced for concerns.

Term 2: The referral system is visibly displayed in staff areas and on noticeboards. It is a regular agenda item at meetings, and staff receive appropriate feedback about the positive impact of referrals.

Term 3: A refresher session on identifying the signs of poor mental health given during directed time. Staff are given data on changes in attendance, punctuality, behaviour and attainment as a result of referrals and subsequent interventions. Pupils are made aware of the support available through assemblies.

Implementing change

Once you have reviewed your current school practices and decided where to set your goals, a degree of change will usually be needed to unite the two. Many factors will affect how easy it will be to introduce change and for it to be accepted. These range from staff morale, the leadership's adaptability and whether there is a discrepancy between the real school culture and leadership's views on it. Some examples of the changes you might implement are bringing in a centralised wellbeing curriculum so that staff aren't duplicating planning (and to ensure a clear sense of progression and cohesion as pupils move up through the years), reconsidering assessment points or bringing in emotional literacy support assistants (ELSAs). You might even incorporate education on mental health and mental wellbeing *within* the curriculum design rather than something that is discretely taught in PSHE, and could potentially be an afterthought due to time constraints. We know of several schools that have integrated mental health into the curriculum, which is a significant, although very worthwhile, change.

Any change, big or small, must begin with communicating *why* the change is needed. No one likes change when it is imposed on them, or when they cannot understand its reasons and therefore may consider it unfair. Consequently, it's essential that whatever leadership approach you take, it is clear that you are passionate about improving the mental health and mental wellbeing of those around you, and that you can clearly communicate your vision and the reasons behind the need for change.

If you wandered into that library filled with leadership books, a large proportion of them would cover implementing change. It is one of the crucial elements of leadership because growth requires innovation. Therefore, as there is already a great deal written on it, we will provide an overview of two effective models for change, beginning with Kotter's 8-step process for leading change. John Kotter, from Harvard Business School, is considered an expert in the field of change; he first published the now classic *Leading Change* in 1996. His model provides insight into the process of 'taking people with you'. Kotter's 8 steps are:

1. Create a sense of urgency by communicating the need for change with all stakeholders so that they see the importance of taking action. This connects with the idea of communicating the *reason* behind needing change.

2. Build a guiding coalition of supportive people with influence who can bring others on board. This reinforces the idea of having governor support and key school leadership members working alongside you.

3. Create a vision that alleviates the natural anxiety that often comes with change. A clear purpose for the change and expected outcomes can ease this anxiety.

4. Communicate the vision to mobilise everyone in the same direction. The vision must be linked to the school's values and mission statement, be highly visible and reinforced at every opportunity to keep it at the forefront of people's minds.

5. Remove barriers such as policies or processes that no longer work, need streamlining and silos (those working in isolation or 'bubbles' such as department teams). Sometimes these barriers can be anticipated; other times, they will emerge during the change process, therefore continually reflecting and responding is key.

6. Generate short-term wins and communicate them. It is important to make progress visible, and share and celebrate it to keep stakeholders motivated.

7. Build on the change by keeping the long-term vision in mind and pushing forward when momentum is increased from early successes.

8. Institute change. This means make it part of the fabric of the institution. It will then become embedded and will replace old habits and ways of doing things. It can be achieved by making connections between the new behaviours and successes.

Another model for change is Kurt Lewin's force field model.[26] This can be particularly useful for addressing Step 5 of Kotter's process, which is removing barriers. Essentially, Lewin's model involves considering the desired change, what driving forces are moving you towards that change and what restraining forces act to prevent it. If the driving forces are equal to the restraining forces, the status quo will be maintained, and no change will occur.

In a school context, driving forces could include improved pupil attendance, behaviour, and attainment. Restraining forces could consist of a lack of staff knowledge, training, or confidence, or too many changes in a short time, leading to staff resistance. Usually, it is the behaviour of others that will alert you to the restraining forces.

To begin applying Lewin's model, define the change you want to see and then list the restraining and driving forces. The next step is to evaluate the forces by asking two questions. Which are the most powerful? And, which might you be able to change? It can often be easier to focus on reducing the restraining forces than increasing the driving forces. Once you've evaluated the forces, you can prioritise action steps to bring about change.

We know that when introducing change, there will always be staff who are enthusiastic, just as there will always be those who are resistant. It can be a valuable exercise to map where the staff fall regarding their openness to change. This will clarify where to focus your efforts when communicating your vision and purpose, and will also highlight key staff members to assist with implementing change.

To help with your reflection on the leadership role, consider the following questions:

1. Which leadership style are you drawn to?
2. Which staff members would you like to include on your team?
3. Which long-term goals are you going to focus on?
4. How can you break these long-term goals down into yearly and termly steps?
5. What changes will you implement?

Summary

✳   The SMHL role is a leadership role that will be made easier with a supportive team.

✳   There are different leadership styles, and the ones that we see regularly used by SMHLs are servant, transformational and authentic leadership.

✳   There are several complementary roles within the school you could consider inviting to join your team. These include the headteacher, deputy head, SENDCo, DSL, local authority virtual head, PSHE lead, heads of year and pastoral staff.

✳   Define your school's best practice approach and choose related, long-term goals.

✳   Prepare the groundwork for implementing change using Kotter's 8 steps, supported by Lewin's force field model if you need to remove barriers to change.

Chapter Six: Looking After Colleagues

'We have prioritised the mental health and wellbeing of children for several years. Our biggest challenge is for the staff to prioritise their own.'
– J.B. (SMHL, Cambridgeshire)

We begin with how to care for and protect colleagues, rather than pupils, for a couple of reasons. The SMHL is in place to *oversee* mental health and mental wellbeing in their school, and they can only implement their policies with the involvement of other staff. In turn, the school's staff cannot implement the procedures to the best of their abilities if their own mental health is poor or their mental wellbeing is strained. Therefore, we begin with them, not only because their mental health is as important as the pupils, but because it is also fundamental to everything that happens in the school.

'Staff' also means every employed adult within the school and does not relate solely to educators. The job of a SMHL is to nurture a culture that is supportive of the mental health and mental wellbeing of *all* staff members, whatever their role—full-time or part-time, educator or facilitator. They are each a member of the school community and, to varying degrees, guardians of the children within their care.

The difficulty when it comes to approaching the mental health of staff for the SMHL is two-fold. Firstly, the SMHL will be aware of the pressures their colleagues face within the school environment (which are often relentless), but they will not necessarily know what is happening in their home lives. Our mental health is affected by all areas of our lives, and staff members might not want to share intimate details of their personal lives with colleagues.

Secondly, we can sometimes fall into the habit of professing 'self-care' as the fix-all, when in reality, teachers often do not have the time to participate in all the things that would aid their mental health. This is a problem that will come up time and again in the education arena. Below we have made some recommendations as to what might help some of your colleagues. These are provided as suggestions rather than answers. What might help one colleague might not work for another, and the idea is to supply them with the information and let them decide for themselves. If the school tries to provide sessions to encourage mental wellbeing, such as yoga or other activities, we must remember that not everyone recharges in the company of others. For some colleagues, extra non-contact time at the end of the working day to acknowledge their contribution will be worth ten 'knit and natter' sessions.

It is a delicate balance between weighing up the needs of your colleagues and the needs of the pupils, and sometimes these can be in conflict. The SMHL will try to do this objectively, even when many of their colleagues are also friends, confidants, and co-workers of many years. We hope that the information below will help when it comes to approaching the mental health and mental wellbeing of the people you work alongside.

Our circle of control

When it comes to our experience of being teachers, 'balance' was a word often used but not often practised for either ourselves or our colleagues. There was little separation between personal and work life, and as SMHL, you will frequently hear about these blended pressures. Life doesn't fit neat little boxes—our work will impact on our home life and vice versa. It all becomes part of the jumble that is just 'life', with its competing pressures. This can feel overwhelming but considering what is within our control and what is not can be a useful tool.

Below is a typical day in the life of a teacher, formed from a combination of our own experiences, those of people we have met along the way, and those of the teachers we train on our SMHL programme. As you read through, it might be helpful to jot down some of the pressures an educator faces, as these are what effective policies and procedures must address. Try to separate them into external circumstances (coming from other people and situations) and internal pressures (coming from the person's own thoughts and feeling about situations).

Alex's story...

I am up and downstairs before the rest of the house is awake. The day will be busy, and I need to get my head in order before the kids wake up. They're usually down by six, so there's no time for yoga this morning. I flick through my planner, which confirms that it will be a chaotic day, as always. First up is an early meeting with the head at 7.30 to talk through my plans for the subject area I'm responsible for.

My husband, Sal, isn't awake yet. He's been panicking about being late for his first meeting because he will have to drop the kids off at school. He's not been himself recently and can sometimes snap at the kids when he's under pressure. I think I'll wake the kids up a bit early so I can make sure they've had breakfast, brushed their teeth, and packed their bags. By the time I leave at seven, all he has to do is make sure they're dressed.

The meeting with the head doesn't go as planned. She's late because of an urgent conversation with the site manager about a dangerous tree that needs to be cordoned off before the pupils arrive. We eventually begin the meeting but are interrupted again—a safeguarding concern needs the head's immediate attention. Our meeting has to be postponed and the morning has been a waste of time.

I quickly prepare for the staff briefing before school, which I now have to run in the head's absence. The atmosphere in the meeting is subdued, and people seem stressed. Running through the agenda, I realise we're adding more to an already heavy workload, but I don't know what I can do about it.

On the way out, I hurry to catch up with a couple of colleagues to ask if they're okay. All they say is, 'yes'. That's that, then. One member of staff, Mike, seems particularly down and has done so for a few weeks. I make a mental note to catch up with him later. Right now, I need to get to the toilet before the bell goes.

Once in the classroom, I manage to have a quick conversation with my teaching assistant before the children come in. There is only enough time to outline the tasks and who I'd like them to work with. As the kids stream into the room, I wish there had been a chance to talk about the children I'm particularly concerned about and discuss the best strategies to support them. The lessons go reasonably well, but I'm not convinced that all the children have done their best work; some of them might be coasting. I spend break time preparing for the next session and manage another quick dash to the toilet.

At lunchtime, I try to find Mike but am cornered by another colleague needing help. I bump into the head, who is very stressed about an impending governor's meeting.

She needs data showing the projected progress for my subject area. I'll have to get it done tonight, so I won't be able to go for the run I was looking forward to.

I start the afternoon lessons without having lunch, but I did manage a cuppa at least. Everyone is tired this afternoon, and motivating the children to complete everything feels like an uphill battle.

After school, I have time for another quick cuppa, and a toilet break before meeting with Logan's parents. I'm not looking forward to it. They want to know why he isn't making more progress and what's being done to support his learning difficulties. I manage to reassure them, but they're not happy, and I know why—he needs more focused 1:1 time, and I need to plan more tasks to support him but haven't had the chance to do this.

I'm late to pick up the kids, but at least they're happy to see me. They tell me they don't want to go to their after-school club anymore because my son is being bullied there. I promise him that I'll speak to the staff tomorrow. I feel terrible. I don't want him going somewhere he's not happy, but who will look after him if he leaves? The evening gets worse. I feel guilty that the children are just watching the telly while I make the tea and do the laundry, and I feel guilty that I'm serving up dinner from the freezer again. I don't think they're getting their 5 a day.

Once the kids are in bed, I start working. When Sal gets home, I say a quick hello but nothing more as I can't break my focus; there's too much to do. I pour a glass of wine and log into my email. My heart sinks. There are 86 unread emails. I begin to plough through them, and my heart sinks further. Mike, the teacher I didn't get to speak to earlier, has been signed off by the doctor with stress and anxiety. The sick note is for three weeks, but I know from experience it will likely be for much longer. He's one of our best teachers, and the children will miss him. I feel responsible. I add 'Find a decent supply' to my task list for tomorrow.

I mark a set of books and put together the report for the head that she wanted. I'm just about to climb the stairs to bed when I remember the laundry that needs hanging out.

My to-do list churns through my head as I try to fall asleep: additional reading to support the proposal for my subject area, additional support for Logan, find a decent supply. The list rolls on... it's going to be another busy day.

This scenario frequently resonates with our senior mental health leads. Whenever any of us encounter this kind of 'day of doom' it can be overwhelming. However, if this is more than an isolated bad day, and becomes systematically repeated, a degree of change is required to tackle it because it will likely negatively impact on both mental health and wellbeing.

Using a circle of control,[27] developed from a model originally created by Stephen Covey can be particularly helpful in these situations. We know that many senior leads on our training programme have used a scenario similar to this during inset and have asked staff to use this tool as a training exercise. It can also be a useful tool for a first aider for mental health to use with a member of staff who is struggling. When considering the above scenario, divide pressure points into three areas. Firstly, those that are within Alex's direct control (the things she can do, think, feel and say without input from others). Secondly, separate those things that are within her influence (what might be affected by what she does, thinks, feels, or says). Finally, notice the things that are outside of both her control and influence but she is still concerned about. By focusing on the elements within our control or influence, we don't expend our energy in a fruitless direction. The idea is that the latter group is the one we should focus less on, eventually aiming to ignore it. Because this is where anxiety takes hold —when we focus on things outside of our control or influence.

Next, consider what Alex could work on that is within her circle of control to address the pressures she faces. This is a useful activity for yourself. It can also be done with staff to encourage them to reflect on their workload and where pressures are coming from. Furthermore, it can be adapted for children or young people by using a different case study or story or even by recording them as they narrate the things they face in their day. If you are interested in this idea, there is more about the circle of control in Covey's *The 7 Habits of Highly Effective People.*

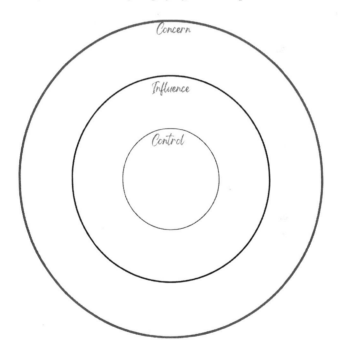

Proactively looking after staff

Assisting staff to look after their mental health and wellbeing is a delicate balance of the proactive and reactive parts of your role. The starting point for the proactive part is that good mental health is not something we either have or don't have—we all fluctuate on a spectrum of health. Therefore, staff's education and access to services must be year-round. As SMHL, you will need to know what aids mental health and wellbeing and how and where people can get help if they feel there is a problem. The proactive part of this role is for staff to have this information so that they can look after themselves in an informed way and so that they can promote and support a positive mental health culture.

Cross industry reports from the Health & Safety Executive published in *Work-related Stress, Depression or Anxiety Statistics in Great Britain*,[28] and updated regularly. have consistently found over half of working days are list due to one of these three conditions. Research referred to in the separate 2018 Whitehall analysis of mental health and wellbeing cited that educating employees about mental health positively impacted wellbeing. However, 74% of respondents to a survey by Education Support[29] said that they didn't feel their initial teacher training prepared them to manage their own wellbeing. Therefore, staff training and development is such a crucial part of any school's strategic plan.

As we have seen from Alex's example above, stress can easily arise in a teaching environment. The Health & Safety Executive defines stress as the *'adverse reaction people have to excessive pressure or other types of demand placed on them'*.[30] The key word here is 'excessive'. Stress in itself is not inherently negative; it is a natural and automatic response. However, excessive or prolonged stress has a toxic effect on the body. Anxiety shares many of the physical symptoms of stress, but while stress is usually a reaction to an external stressor, anxiety is an internal anticipation of a perceived threat or danger.

The long-term effects of prolonged and excessive stress can include depression, anxiety, personality disorders, high blood pressure, heart disease or stroke, problems with the immune system and problems with the digestive system. Therefore, it's crucial within a school to challenge a culture of busyness and the badge of honour, 'first in, last to leave' (which is frankly one of the many creations of the 1980s that should remain there).

To support staff mental health and resilience, it's essential to know how stress levels can be managed in a healthy way. It is also important to consider some of the less helpful 'quick fixes' that could negatively affect mental health and wellbeing. It is common for people to turn to quick fixes for mental health, like the glass of wine Alex has at the end of the night. Although this could help wellbeing in the moment, it might add to the stresses of the next day.

Self-medicating refers to using alcohol, illegal drugs, or prescription drugs as a coping mechanism to relieve symptoms of sadness and not being able to cope. Alcohol is one of the most common substances used because it is legal in the UK and easy to obtain. While self-medicating may provide immediate relief of symptoms such as anxiety, this is only temporary. Alcohol and other drugs can adversely change the brain's chemistry, which can worsen the symptoms of mental illness if it is already present and can cause mental illness if used excessively.

Although healthy coping strategies do not have such an instant effect, they have longer-term benefits. To achieve long-lasting mental wellbeing, we must look after ourselves in the moment while simultaneously looking after our future selves as well.

In 2008, the Foresight Mental Capital and Well-being Project commissioned the New Economics Foundation (NEF) to develop 'Five Ways to Wellbeing'[31]—as a parallel to the 'five fruits and vegetables a day'. This work provided the evidence-base which was subsequently adopted by the NHS as the recommended guidance for improving mental health and wellbeing. The five elements are:

- **Connect**: Spend time with people who are important to you and develop these relationships.
- **Be active**: Excessive stress hormones create an energy surge, and physical activity can be a good way of using them. Something as simple as going for a walk has been shown to improve wellbeing.
- **Keep learning**: Learning new skills leads to a sense of

achievement and increased self-confidence. It's also good to nurture interests that are nothing to do with work to help with a sense of a balanced and well-rounded life.

- **Give to others**: Even small things, like letting someone go in front of you at the photocopier, can make a difference to others and also give you the feeling that you are contributing to something bigger and that your actions make a difference.
- **Be mindful**: Mindfulness can include meditation but is not limited to this. It is about fully engaging your senses to connect the mind with the body, rather than 'living in your head'.

The above is the basis of the information that needs to be passed across to staff, but some thought must be given to how it is conveyed. For example, sitting down busy staff to talk about ways they can look after their mental health before their classes begin might not be well received. They might interpret it as bad for their mental health to attend yet another meeting when they've got many other things to do—we've all felt the irony when it comes to well-intentioned but clumsily delivered wellbeing initiatives. Therefore, we need to think about alternative ways of getting that information across. You might decide on a training session that forms part of an inset day or use noticeboards or weekly wellbeing bulletins. This will be a judgement call depending on the culture of your school.

The school culture is so influential when it comes to the mental health and wellbeing of staff members. Of course, stress is not just caused by work, as personal factors can also impact individuals, but when we spend so many hours of our day in a work environment, that environment has to be considered. Ideally, if they are not already in place, steps should be taken to even out the pressure points within the school year (as discussed in Chapter 2) and then protected in the mental health policy. Things such as a staff member being able to attend their own child's nativity or going to the dentist, help staff feel that the school is assisting in making their lives work for them. Fundamentally, this supportive culture can prevent issues from occurring further down the line.

Reactively looking after staff

Even in the most nurturing, supportive, well-informed school environment, there will still be cases of poor mental health or mental wellbeing among staff that are flagged to the SMHL. This is inevitable because mental health is affected by a combination of factors, not just a work environment. Depending on the size of your school and the school environment, your input might be required on a weekly (sometimes daily) basis. Another colleague, such as the head, might request your input, or you might spot signs of poor mental health in a staff member.

If we take the case of Mike in the earlier scenario who was signed off from work by his doctor, how would Alex react to this if she was the SMHL? Ultimately, the SMHL is not responsible for the wellbeing of individual staff members. Instead, their oversight role encompasses putting protective factors in place, developing a supportive culture, and making sure that staff know where to turn when they experience difficulties. This is different to taking on responsibility for someone else's wellbeing. Creating a reasonable workload and a protective work environment is an employer's responsibility; however, managing wellbeing at an individual level is the responsibility of the individual (although school leadership can, and should, offer support). The role of the SMHL is to contribute to and communicate knowledge about the systems and processes that both the employer and the individual have available in their decision making. So, in the case of Mike, the SMHL can only try to put things in place that will be supportive, such as signposting and flagging things up to the head teacher and possibly to whoever is in charge in a HR capacity.

However, the SMHL could potentially approach Mike directly if they are also a first aider for mental health. This would require additional training, as it is outside the approved SMHL course. This separate qualification would train the SMHL in how to have a supportive conversation with Mike and they will know the parameters and structure of that conversation. It would have to be approached sensitively as Mike might not want to talk to anyone, so having this structure in place means you will not overstep boundaries. Having well publicised first aiders for mental health and their available times displayed can encourage staff to seek help. Posting details on a noticeboard of confidential counselling services, such as those offered by the charity Education Support, or the contact numbers for well-being services your school may have bought into, can do the same.

Training as a mental health first aider is an invaluable additional qualification to have as SMHL and for other members of staff in the SMHL's team. It is the equivalent of a one-day course for a Level 2 qualification or a two-day course for a more advanced Level 3 qualification. Several organisations provide this training, including ours, and it can be split into ninety-minute sessions at the end of the school day, so you don't have to take an entire day or two out of your schedule.

The second way you might be involved reactively is when another colleague flags a situation that requires your input. You may, in some circumstances, be able to work out a route to resolve the issue that doesn't impact anyone, but quite often, you will be faced with an ethical dilemma where not everyone involved will be happy with the outcome. There are several ways you can approach ethical dilemmas, and we will discuss this in Chapter 8 when we review the pupil dilemma raised in the first chapter.

For the moment, consider the following scenario and how you, as SMHL, would approach it in a way that has the least impact on everyone involved:

Case Study

Nikolai has worked at the school for thirty years and is currently deputy head. Over the last five years, Nik has gone through some dark times with his marriage breakdown and poor physical health. This has taken its toll on his mental health, and he has been very open about this. Recently, he has approached the head for support, and adjustments have been made to his responsibilities to ease the pressure on him.

As the school is a small village primary school, Nik has a job share with another teacher in the Year 5/6 class. This includes preparing the children for KS2 SATs. Although he has always been an effective classroom teacher, over the past year or so, lesson drop-ins and book looks show that the quality of teaching is not of his usual standard and, in comparison to the other class teachers, is not as impactful for the children. Support staff in the room are complaining that they don't know what to prepare as planning is not shared, and this worries them as their own performance depends on the teacher being clear about the aims for the lesson and individual students.

In his deputy role, Nik is performing well and has recently seemed brighter in himself, thanking staff regularly for their support through tough times.

The head is at a loss for what to do as she has worked with Nik for many years. She is relieved he is feeling better, but issues remain. She asks you as the SMHL for advice.

When we have discussed scenarios like this one with groups of SMHLs, most have concluded that there are ways to navigate such situations that can lead to good outcomes for all. However, it requires careful thought and a sensitive approach to make this happen, which can be aided by having a close team with whom you can discuss such situations in confidence.

For Nik's scenario, we suggest approaching it with compassion and honesty. Nik has already opened the lines of communication by discussing the problems he has faced. We believe that, in return, he deserves an honest approach rather than everyone proceeding to discuss his situation behind his back (which, if he found out, would also likely impact his mental health). Advising the head to approach Nik, with or without the SMHL lead, and raising that Nik still needs some support with his classroom work is a response that brings a degree of dignity to the situation.

Honesty is often labelled as 'brutal', but honesty can be kind, especially when specific, rather than lumping in every complaint or possible issue. So, rather than approaching Nik and saying there is an issue with his classroom teaching, approach him and instead say there is an issue with 'X' in the classroom and pick out one thing at a time. Being clear is kind. Then gaps between where things are and where they need to be can be addressed openly, supportively and as a team. That builds trust and a culture of psychological safety. Something else to consider is that if Nik is doing well in his role as a deputy, what are his goals and aspirations? Does he still want to be a classroom teacher? Maybe this is something worth exploring with him. One thing we frequently emphasise on our first aid for mental health courses is that we should never make assumptions. Asking open questions and listening fully to the responses is more appropriate than trying to 'fix' things for someone.

Fundamentally, looking after staff wellbeing will aid student wellbeing as staff will be more able, and likely, to engage with pupils' mental health. This relationship is bidirectional in that one of the protective factors of mental health as an educator is the sense of purpose you feel and the impact you can have on young people.

Before we move on to pupil mental health in the next chapter, consider the following questions:

1. What is within your circle of control in the SMHL role?
2. What is within your circle of influence in the SMHL role?
3. What is outside your circle of control in the SMHL role?
4. What would you like to focus on in the short term that is within your circle of control?
5. Considering the *Five Ways to Well-being*, what element might you need to address when it comes to your own wellbeing?

Summary

✸ Staff mental health and wellbeing impacts the school culture and pupils' wellbeing.

✸ Mental health and wellbeing are affected by multiple factors in our personal and professional lives.

✸ To help reduce poor mental health, the SMHL needs to provide information to staff members on what promotes mental wellbeing and what short-term fixes might not assist it in the long term.

✸ The SMHL will also need to act in a reactive way when concerns are raised about members of staff either from their own observations or when concerns are raised by the SLT etc.

✸ These situations and ethical dilemmas will often not have a right or wrong answer, so having a supervisor or a team to discuss situations in confidence with is essential.

Chapter Seven: How Staff Can Look After Pupils

'Staff are already well versed in looking for signs of safeguarding concerns so I think following the same process in terms of mental health is a useful prompt for them.'
– K.W. (SMHL, Surrey)

With nearly 300 pupils in an average primary school and 950 in an average secondary school,[32] where does a SMHL begin when it comes to monitoring and aiding the mental health of all of these pupils? We suggest by reminding yourself that the SMHL is not responsible for each individual pupil's mental health. Instead, what they *are* responsible for is to impart training to staff who have direct daily contact with pupils, which the SMHL could never feasibly do.

When faced with an already pressurised schedule, it is understandable that educators may view the added responsibility of pupils' mental health and wellbeing as a struggle. How will they fit it in on top of everything else? As SMHL, the way to approach these busy schedules is to make it as easy as possible for staff to learn essential information, be aware of the signs of poor mental health and know the procedures in place to raise a concern. If you make it simple for staff to engage and implement effective systems, then you have successfully achieved a large part of your role.

Information for staff

For any school that wants to establish a positive mental health culture, it is essential that staff are trained to recognise the signs and symptoms of mental health needs in pupils and what to do if they have concerns. The benefits of training include increased staff confidence and bringing mental health in line with procedures for safeguarding. Ideally, staff should receive annual training (with top-up training later in the school year) on identifying mental health concerns and referring these to the SMHL.

Staff nomination is the most common method of identifying children who might be struggling with their mental health.[33] In this case, a staff member will flag up a child to the SMHL if they have concerns about them. However, for this to be effective, staff must be aware of the behaviours that can indicate poor mental health in pupils.[34] In many instances these behaviours may also be indicators of a safeguarding concern, which again highlights why the close working relationship between the SMHL and the DSL is so vital. It is important for staff to be aware that for some pupils, the behavioural indicators might not be as obvious and there are pupils who will internalise their distress.

Behavioural indicators can include:

- Constant fidgeting
- Getting out of their seat
- Struggling to focus for prolonged periods
- Being disorganised
- Missing instructions from staff
- Being verbally or physically abusive

- Destroying property
- Leaving class or truanting
- Stealing
- Arguing with authority figures
- Refusing to follow instructions
- Aiming to distract others through inappropriate behaviour
- Not completing classwork or homework, whereas previously they did
- Becoming irritated easily and arguing with others
- Being persistently tired or sleepy
- Having a negative self-image
- Not participating in activities they used to enjoy
- Consistent lateness
- Poor attendance

There are also risk factors for pupils developing mental health issues that staff should be made aware of. These include:

- A long-term physical illness
- A parent who has had problems with mental health, drugs or alcohol use, or who has been in trouble with the law
- Experiencing the death of someone close
- Parents who separate or divorce
- Being severely bullied
- Physically or sexually abused
- Living in poverty or being homeless
- Experiencing discrimination, perhaps because of their race, LGBTQIA+ identity, disability, being neuro-atypical

(e.g. having autism or ADHD), gender or religion and the impact of intersectionality
- Acting as a carer for a relative or taking on adult responsibilities
- Having long-standing educational difficulties
- Being labelled as 'clever' and developing perfectionist tendencies
- Excessive gaming or use of social media
- Insufficient sleep over a sustained period
- Poor diet over a sustained period

When sharing this information, we suggest coupling it with the statistics below, which often helps grab people's attention as they highlight how prevalent some of these circumstances are. In an average-sized class:[35]

- Ten children would have witnessed their parents separate
- Eight will have experienced severe physical violence, sexual abuse or neglect
- Seven will have been bullied
- One will have experienced the death of a parent

Some more statistics for you to share that we find very impactful are:

- Only one in eight children who have been sexually abused will come to the attention of the authorities[36]
- Up to a quarter of teenagers have experienced violence in their intimate partner relationships[37]
- 1 in 10 children aged 5–16 have a diagnosable mental health condition[38]
- Half of all mental health problems are established by the age of fourteen[39]
- Three-quarters of all mental health problems are established by the age of twenty-four[40]

You might also want to include in your training the signs and symptoms of mental health conditions that educators are likely to encounter in schools or colleges. We have chosen the six that we discuss most regularly with the SMHLs who train with us. While it is vital for the SMHL and staff members to be aware of these conditions, this is not so that they can diagnose or treat them. Instead, it is so that they are aware of the signs and symptoms and feel able to refer pupils to appropriate help. The job of the SMHL, and the educators that they train, is one of observing, and the key is to notice change. Educators know their young people as they spend hours with them each week, so changes in their usual demeanour will be more apparent to them than to a new counsellor, for instance.

- **Anxiety:** Signs of anxiety include being unable to relax, constantly on edge, irritable, and having trouble concentrating. Because it is associated with the same hormones as stress, it physically affects the body. Symptoms can include feeling breathless or dizzy, sweating, trembling, racing heart, chest pains, or muscle aches, and pains. Social withdrawal can be a sign of anxiety, as can seeking constant reassurance.
- **Depression:** Signs of depression include irritability and being intolerant of others, changes in appetite leading to weight gain or loss, a lack of energy, muscle aches and pains, persistent low mood, disturbed sleep, tearfulness, and a lack of motivation or interest in anything.
- **Self-harm:** Signs of self-harm are unexplained cuts and bruises, low self-esteem, depression, keeping covered even in hot weather, and claiming to have frequent accidents or mishaps. (If you suspect someone is self-harming, it is important not to tell them to 'just stop' because self-harm is often a coping mechanism or a way of relieving distressing emotions. If someone stops abruptly, without professional support to find other, healthier coping strategies, it could cause further issues. There is a lot of overlap with safeguarding here, so working closely with the DSL is essential.)

- **Eating disorders**: Signs that someone could be struggling with an eating disorder include lying about how much they've eaten, being secretive about eating, anxiety around eating, eating very quickly, going to the bathroom immediately after eating, obsessive exercising, or cutting food into small pieces and eating very slowly. Sudden and dramatic weight loss can also be a sign of an eating disorder, but it's important to remember that many people with eating disorders might be a normal weight or overweight. (If you suspect someone has an eating disorder, it is best not to raise your concerns about them around mealtimes and don't broach the topic of food directly with them. Instead, ask them general, open questions about how they are feeling.)
- **Psychosis**: Psychosis is an altered perception of reality. A person might see, hear, or experience things that others do not. This can manifest as hallucinations—visual or auditory are the most common, but these can also relate to other senses such as smell, taste, or touch. Other signs or symptoms include suspiciousness, confused or disturbed thoughts, delusions, lack of self-awareness, depression and anxiety, dark thoughts, and disturbed sleep. Psychosis can occur in response to events (for example, post-partum psychosis or as a result of drugs or alcohol or withdrawal from substances). It can also be part of a long-term mental health condition, such as schizophrenia. Either way, the symptoms of psychosis can be frightening for the person experiencing them and for those around them. The sooner someone receives professional help, the better their outcomes, so signposting swiftly is essential.
- **Suicide**: The term suicide covers a range of different things a person may be experiencing. Suicidal ideation refers to thoughts of suicide which can either be active (plans are made) or passive (no plans are made). Some people attempt suicide, which means they intend to take their own life but it doesn't result in death. Clinicians will use tools to identify

the level of risk to a person but in a school context, our job is to look out for signs that aid timely intervention and treatment if required. These signs might include threatening to hurt or kill themselves, self-harm, feeling hopeless or directionless, talking about being a burden to others, talking or writing about death or suicide, recent trauma, increased use of alcohol or drugs, social withdrawal, or bereavement. If someone has a family member who has taken their own life, they have an increased risk of dying by suicide. When we talk about suicide, we don't use the phrase 'commit suicide' anymore as this refers to the time it was classed as a crime, and the term carries stigma and judgement. Instead, we say someone 'took their own life' or 'died by suicide'.

If one of the ways of highlighting concerns is through staff observation, we should also encourage fostering a relationship of trust where pupils feel they can share their concerns. It is helpful if staff have, or build, relationships with pupils that encourage openness and in which a pupil sees their teacher as an adult with whom they can share their worries and concerns. Persuading staff to engage and interact with students on a more personal level, to show warmth and openness through interactions outside of the classroom, or to allow them to miss lessons to access support can be seen as a challenge in some contexts. The inclusive approach set by the SMHL, and providing staff training, are ways to overcome this barrier.

Information for students

The other side to protecting pupils' mental health and wellbeing is teaching them about this through either a programme of PSHE or within the curriculum itself. The entire contents of what should be covered could fill a book, so we will just touch on a few key concepts. Firstly, it's important to consider where in the curriculum the school covers mental health and mental illness. This may be done as a discrete PSHE session or something that is more regularly discussed. Visual representations can work well here to convey information that is sometimes challenging to absorb, such as diagrams that show, for instance, how the parasympathetic and sympathetic nervous systems work.

Where mental health is addressed in PSHE is also important. We have previously discussed the links between physical and mental health. As pupils will probably already be learning about physical health in PSHE, this is an excellent place to insert mental health as they are interwoven concepts, which is often unclear to young people. Also, many view physical health as more important than mental health without fully considering the co-dependency between the two. One way to teach about this is to hold a design competition where you ask the children and young people to create a design to represent the idea that our physical and mental health are linked.

This learning within classes can then be supported in the broader school culture by addressing it in assemblies or designating times to discuss it. The key aspects of what aids mental wellbeing, that we discussed in the previous chapter, will also have to be conveyed, but there is one necessary word of caution. Even though the information around self-care is invaluable, as writer and researcher Nakita Valerio poignantly put it, *'Shouting "self care!" at people who actually need "community care" is how we fail people.'*[41] While schools and colleges cannot 'fix' all of society's ills, with the proper knowledge, training, and systems, they can have a positive impact and be part of the wider solution.

The way information is presented in communications by schools is also part of their commitment to mental health in the community. As a respected source of information, the language schools use can greatly impact the knowledge and attitudes of students and families. You may wish to consider how you convey mental health in your communications. By signing up to the Mental Health Media Charter,[42] a school will signal that they are committed to discussing and reporting stories relating to mental health responsibly, helpfully in a way that considers the needs of the most vulnerable members of the population. The charter states, in part, that signatories will do their best not to:

1. Use the phrase 'commit suicide' or 'successful suicide'. The best alternative for this is 'died by suicide'. Other options are

'attempted/complete suicide' or 'took/ended their own life'.

2. Show 'before' images in eating disorder stories or pictures that could trigger people who self-harm.

3. Use the terms 'anorexics', 'bulimics', 'depressives', 'schizophrenics', etc.

4. Give too much detail on suicide/self-harm or eating disorder methodology.

5. Use generic terms like 'mental health issues' when describing terrorists and other violent criminals.

Sadly, some studies have shown that the risks of copycat behaviour when a suicide is in the media are real and this is known as the 'The Werther Effect'. However, other studies have suggested that when constructive coping strategies and solutions are presented in the reporting, this can have a preventative outcome. This phenomenon is known as the 'Papageno Effect'.[43] For educators, this emphasises the importance of the work schools do as a counterbalance to what young people may be exposed to elsewhere.

If you know that the content of your messaging supports good mental health, then the final thing to consider is *how* it is conveyed. One of the most challenging and delicate aspects of being a SMHL is knowing how to share knowledge in an impactful way with staff and the student body, without it being overwhelming and negatively received. For the final part of these two sections, consider your own setting and think about the pros and cons of each of the following methods of communication:

Methods of communication

- Modelling of the behaviours you wish to see in small working groups

- Regular update emails

- Posters on shared boards

> ✼   A regular slot in a staff meeting
>
> ✼   Visuals around school or college
>
> ✼   Sharing of case-studies
>
> ✼   Briefing of staff regarding individual students

ACEs and the DSL

Many of the risk factors mentioned earlier in this chapter for developing a mental health condition are also referred to as Adverse Childhood Experiences (ACEs). ACEs are highly stressful events in childhood that are potentially traumatic for the individual.

ACEs are relatively common, with 67% of the population experiencing at least one ACE. However, for those who suffer four or more, there is an increased risk of being involved in substance abuse, unintended teenage pregnancy, the victim or perpetrator of violence, prison sentences, disease, disability, and ultimately an increased risk of early death.[44] That is because multiple ACEs result in toxic stress, the prolonged activation of the stress response, which in turn results in what is called a fixed allostatic load. If we imagine each person having their own stress thermostat, too many ACEs can lead to a child's stress thermostat being permanently on high. As a result of this fixed allostatic load, the nervous system rarely has a chance to return to a calm state, which can have a damaging effect on the body and brain.

If we look back at the external and internal signs of poor mental health, such as outbursts of anger and an inability to concentrate, with the right training in place, staff will hopefully view these as a potential symptom of something else happening in the child's life. The information above should be passed to staff because if we can identify ACEs and intervene early enough, we can help reset that thermostat. This will not only help the child at the time, but the adult they will become and any children they might have, as the research around ACEs suggests a generational cycle.

Schools are becoming more aware of the impact of ACEs, and the statistic about the effect of four or more ACEs is relatively widespread. However, we must remember the involvement of toxic stress with ACEs, as this is key. A child who suffers an acute or isolated stressful event might not have the repeated triggering of their stress response that another child will experience who lives within a household where the stress is chronic, such as in the case of domestic violence or sexual abuse. When a child doesn't feel safe in their home, they will be hypervigilant, and their body and mind will never have the chance to calm down, resulting in this chronic stress.

Another thing you have probably spotted is that many ACEs are also safeguarding concerns. Therefore, as SMHL, (unless you fill both roles) you will have to refer safeguarding concerns over to the DSL when they arise. There is often an overlap between the concerns of the two roles, and the DSL should also refer pupils with mental health needs to the SMHL. An ideal scenario within a school is that the DSL and SMHL work closely together to support pupils strategically from both arenas.

Information about pupils should be shared between the DSL and SMHL. However, there may be cases where the DSL does not feel that they should be sharing this information because the SMHL is outside of the 'need to know basis'. It is to be hoped that, following the DfE's investment in raising the profile of the SMHL to a similar expert level as the DSL, information about the background or experiences of a pupil with potential mental health concerns is considered something a SMHL needs to know.

Firstly, if someone is experiencing something that amounts to a safeguarding issue, this may have also impacted their mental health. The SMHL can support this pupil with internal interventions and external referrals. By not telling the SMHL, the pupil is being further isolated. Secondly, if this pupil approaches the SMHL, they will have to explain their situation again, which might be detrimental to their mental health. A more joined-up approach would be for the SMHL to have all the information they need so they can concentrate on helping the pupil rather than the pupil having to repeatedly explain the thing that is hurting them. The pupil's overall needs should always come first. Ultimately, if the sharing of information cannot be agreed, it is up to the head to decide on how much should be divulged, but good practice is that the DSL and SMHL

work closely for the good of the children and that the systems and processes around confidentiality are designed to carefully accommodate this
professional working relationship.

Monitoring students' mental health and mental wellbeing

As well as staff nominating pupils to the SMHL, the SMHL can take proactive steps to consider the pupils' mental health within their school. These
steps can also help monitor the impact of interventions that have been put
in place, which we will talk more about in the next chapter.

The first step that can help monitor pupils' mental health is screening
and there are various types that could be used. Many feel passionately that
there should be universal screening to monitor the wellbeing of the school
over time. The benefit of this approach is that it lessens the chance of pupils falling through the net. However, there is a cost implication to this
that the SLT would have to approve as serious consideration would need
to be given to who conducts the process and how the data is used. This is
not something that should be undertaken lightly.

Some professionals favour targeted screening, where children are assessed when a concern is raised. This concern may come from staff nomination, pupil or staff referral, or behavioural issues. At this stage, we must
consider how the SMHL assesses a pupil's mental health when they are
brought to their attention and how they act on the outcome of any screening that takes place.

A range of different approaches to screening are used in schools and
we discuss some of the most widely used methods below.

Validated surveys

Validated surveys are tested on representative samples and have been
shown to have adequate reliability and validity. The Child Outcomes Research Consortium (CORC)[45] offers validated surveys to provide wellbeing measurements to schools from years 4–11, and staff surveys as well.

They assess mental health, emotional wellbeing, and resilience across the school, providing an effective universal screening method. The results can assist in identifying areas where pupils might need support, and follow-up surveys can help evaluate the steps to provide that support. For targeted screening the Strengths and Difficulties Questionnaire (SDQ) and the Boxall Profile are often used in schools.

Strengths and difficulties questionnaire (SDQ)

The SDQ[46] is a short behavioural screening questionnaire for children aged 3 to 16. It is used to assess children's mental health, screen for poor mental health, and evaluate the outcomes of interventions. They are used in clinical and educational settings and can be completed by children and young people, their parents, or teachers. Because of this, the SDQ can be used to seek feedback from staff and to help families understand how mental health issues could impact their child's behaviour and attendance. In addition, studies have shown that the SDQ demonstrates the effects of treatment, so it can be used to evaluate the impact of everyday practice (for example, in clinics or special schools) or to assess the effects of specific interventions with individuals or small groups. Research has shown that the SDQ may be used with children and young people with mild learning difficulties but not with more severe learning difficulties.[47]

Boxall Profile

The Boxall Profile[48] is another method for identification and monitoring. It assesses social, emotional, and mental health needs and provides a standardised emotional literacy score. It therefore helps with early identification and assessment, as well as target setting, intervention, and monitoring progress. It is made up of a two-part checklist, which is completed by a staff member who knows the young person best. It also identifies the level of the child's skills to access learning and sets individualised, achievable targets for social and emotional aptitudes, which are reviewed and re-assessed periodically.

Finally, schools could also identify possible mental health problems by monitoring school data and noticing changes in pupils' attainment patterns, attendance, or behaviour. We have already touched on this relating to staff members nominating children whose behaviour is a cause for concern. However, this can also be identified by pastoral leads or someone with an overview of behavioural incidents. As the SMHL, it is vital to work closely with members of the leadership team responsible for behaviour and familiar with the school's behaviour policy.

In the next chapter, we will consider what in-school interventions the SMHL can take both to promote good mental health and wellbeing and to respond to needs as identified by screening. For the moment, consider your own school's approach to educating staff and pupils around mental health and answer the following questions:

1. In which areas do staff need training in relation to mental health and wellbeing? (For example, what mental health is, the impact of stress, strategies to manage stress, how to identify mental health needs in students, what to do if they identify a need, etc.)
2. How do you know that staff need training in these areas?
3. How will staff be trained? (As a whole group, in smaller groups according to need, using a coaching model, etc.)
4. How much time will be allocated for this training?
5. How will you disseminate the required information for staff development? (Formal training sessions, lunch and learn sessions, newsletters, emails, noticeboards, etc.)

Summary

* One of the key ways schools can be alert to possible concerns about pupils' mental health is with the involvement of trained staff notifying the SMHL of a change in a pupil's behaviour.

* Staff should be trained in the signs of poor mental health and the risk factors for developing mental health needs.

* Pupils should also be educated about mental health in PSHE or as part of the curriculum. When approaching children's education, it is important to consider the language and phrases used.

* Ideally, the SMHL and the DSL will work in a close partnership of referral and support. Staff should be aware of ACEs and their potential impact on children's futures.

* Students' mental health can be screened either in a universal or targeted manner. Consideration needs to be given to ensuring the process is planned carefully. Monitoring school data and noticing changes in pupils' patterns of attainment, attendance and behaviour can also flag pupils who may be of concern.

Chapter Eight: In-school Support

'We want the response to be clearly understood by all stakeholders so that support can be given quickly and effectively for the child. I particularly liked the idea of including self-referral and pupil referral so we will be including these too.'
– N.N. (SMHL, Lancashire)

Before going into the specifics of what support and interventions can take place, let's step up onto the banks of our islands to survey the school from this vantage point. It is from here that we should hopefully view the thriving ecosystem that has evolved and how it offers an intricate framework of support for pupils. Ideally, everyone contributes to a shared system where they make decisions for themselves while being considerate to others and mindful of their impact. This is held together by a clear ethos or vision for the school, which surrounds everyone and pulls them together.

A shared vision creates a culture where students want to behave in a certain way. Rather than relying solely on rules and regulations, it's about clarity of expectation around how we treat each other. This will then be reflected in a behaviour policy or approach to behaviour. Clear, consistent expectations create an ethos, and with this ethos comes a sense of belonging and usually a desire to belong. Autonomous moral reasoning will hopefully become second nature to most pupils and smooth their transition into wider society. Therefore, creating a flourishing school system is an intervention in itself.

System of referrals

A clear and consistent approach to behaviour across the school, with staff using the same system and approaches, helps support those pupils who find the expected social norms and routines challenging. It also helps identify those who regularly struggle with the school's behavioural expectations.

Of course, non-compliance with the behaviour policy is just one of many routes that a pupil will come to your attention as SMHL. The other routes were discussed in the previous chapter and primarily consist of staff nomination, screening, and changes in attainment and attendance. It's essential to have well-communicated channels through which staff (whether teaching, pastoral, or associate) can refer concerns to the SMHL once a potential need is identified—similar to how safeguarding concerns are referred to the DSL. This system should also incorporate access for pupils and parents to refer matters and any procedure should allow pupils to seek support confidentially.

Once a student is identified as having a need, the graduated response of assess, plan, do, and review is an effective next step. This method is not new to teachers and permeates all aspects of school life. The graduated response offered in the SEND code of practice[49] provides a framework for deciding what support to offer and is considered best practice for responding to mental health needs, whether or not they constitute a special educational need.

- **Assess**: This is an all-encompassing approach to gathering information from various sources. It will include speaking to the pupil, their parent or guardian, and any relevant teachers. Data such as behavioural records, progress and attainment, as well as attendance and punctuality, should also be analysed.

- **Plan**: The support plan should be evidence-based and provide staff with the skills and knowledge to implement it. This should address specific adjustments or interventions and explain the expected changes or impact. It should also include a review date. The pupil's parents may be shown the plan where appropriate and have an opportunity to share their views (this will be a judgement call in some situations and liaison with the DSL may be necessary).

- **Do**: Classroom teachers will need to be supported in implementing the identified strategies or approaches during their teaching and have the skills to assess their impact.

- **Review**: This should happen on the agreed date to evaluate the impact of interventions against expectations. The views of the pupil (and parents, where appropriate) should also be sought. The support plan will then be revised, if necessary, with regular reviews scheduled.

It's essential to know all the possible adjustments and interventions available within the school and through the statutory and independent mental health services in your area, such as the local services listed in the transformation plans covered in Chapter 2. Statutory support for mental health problems for all children and young people is based on a tier system:

Tier 1:   Universal mental health and wellbeing interventions provided by professionals who do not specialise in mental health, i.e., teachers.

Tier 2   Mental health services provided by practitioners who specialise in mental health, i.e., counsellors and Mental Health Support Teams.

Tier 3:   Specialist and young people's mental health services, i.e., CYPMHS.

Tier 4   Inpatient or highly specialised mental health services for conditions such as eating disorders.

Tier 1 will be covered in more detail in this chapter, and Tiers 2, 3, and 4 in the next one. In most schools, the majority of support offered to pupils in relation to mental health and wellbeing will be non-clinical interventions that support mental health.

It can be helpful to visualise your school population in a funnel shape. Most students—arguably all—will benefit from some Tier 1 practices plus any whole-school interventions you put in place. The next level down, which is still Tier 1, is where some pupils may benefit from targeted support in schools. This could be working with a pastoral member of staff, doing suggested activities that may positively impact their mental health or some small group work.

There will be students who require Tier 2 support, which is the option to work with a trained professional, for example a counsellor or art therapist. You may have these professionals in your school or as part of your trust, you may be able to access them through your local offer (outlined in your local transformation plan) or Mental Health Support Teams, or the school may choose to direct funds—such as the pupil premium funding—into paying for a private practitioner to support specific students.

Where Tier 1 and 2 support has been insufficient, some students will require referral to Tier 3 services, which in turn may refer to Tier 4 support. This level of support is designed to treat children and young people with the most severe or complex mental health difficulties, which on average accounts for only 2% of children. Consequently, the majority of children who present with mental health concerns will be sufficiently supported with Tier 1 or Tier 2 interventions.

It should always be remembered that if staff have a mental health concern that is also a safeguarding concern, immediate action should be taken by following the school's safeguarding policy and via the designated safeguarding lead.

At present, there is no national threshold to demarcate these tiers, that is, in England as a whole, there is no definitive description of which indicators place a child in which tier. Instead, the thresholds are area specific. A few local authorities have created their own documents outlining thresholds based on the 'Thrive Model'.[50] It would be helpful to create one for your school if you don't already have one. The best place to start would be to contact your local CYPMHS to find out whether they have any available threshold guidance.

Tier 1: Informal and formal in-school support

Tier 1 focuses on non-clinical interventions to support mental health. It is likely many of these are already in place in your school, whether you are aware of them or not. If you have not got one already, it's worth creating a database or list of what your school already provides. These can be separated into informal and formal support. Which bracket it would fall into would depend on whether the provision would be recorded in a pupil's records and its impact monitored. Additionally, informal interventions are universally available and pupils who have not been referred may also attend, which would not necessarily be recorded unless the staff member keeps a register. Suggestions of informal and formal in-school support are:

100 Intervention Ideas

Informal Interventions

Connect

1. Buddy reading
2. Wellbeing drop-ins
3. Quiet reading spaces
4. Library visits
5. Lunchtime groups
6. Choirs
7. School trips
8. Informal study sessions
9. Casual conversation between staff and pupils
10. Guest speakers
11. Tea and biscuit breaktimes
12. Anti-bullying programmes
13. Life skills sessions
14. Social Media clinics
15. Languages clubs
16. An open-door policy with a member of staff trained in child mental health

Take Notice

17. Window box monitors
18. Bird watching
19. Meditation
20. Qi Gong
21. Wellbeing spot checks
22. Gratitude journalling
23. Star gazing club
24. Vision boarding sessions
25. Brain breaks
26. Wellbeing planning
27. Self-care guidance
28. Colouring sessions
29. Visualisation activities
30. Hama beading groups
31. Support with personal organisation
32. Nature walks

Give

33. Sponsored events
34. School pet duties
35. Pensioner visits
36. Helping at open evenings
37. Eco responsibilities
38. Homework support buddies
39. Food bank collections
40. Fundraising committees
41. Assembly teams
42. Volunteering opportunities
43. Random acts of kindness
44. 365 day giving challenge as a group
45. Walk and talk sessions
46. Leadership roles for pupils
47. Oratory opportunities
48. Playtime buddies

Be Active:

49. Walking lunches
50. Gardening
51. Martial arts
52. Boxing
53. Tai Chi
54. Skipping challenge
55. Yoga sessions
56. Football club
57. Hockey club
58. Rugby club
59. Netball club
60. Tennis club
61. Gym club
62. Dance club
63. Couch to 5K
64. Bushcraft and forest school activities

Keep Learning:

65. Chess clubs and tournaments
66. Art and Design clubs
67. Board game sessions
68. Debate clubs
69. Music sessions
70. Drama opportunities
71. Cookery clubs
72. Warhammer club
73. Minecraft club
74. Book club
75. Crossword sessions
76. Sudoku sessions
77. Teenage brain sessions
78. YoYo challenge
79. Rubik's cube challenge
80. Maths challenges

Formal Interventions

(Some of the above informal interventions could also become a formal intervention if planned, targeted and the outcomes are evaluated and recorded for each child.)

81. Emotional literacy workshops
82. Growth mindset sessions
83. ELSA interventions
84. Positive Psychology techniques
85. Social and Emotional Skills-based interventions
86. Mental health literacy activities
87. Mindfulness sessions
88. Coaching (teacher to pupil or pupil to pupil) or coaching skills sessions
89. Mentoring schemes (teacher to pupil or pupil to pupil)
90. First Aid for Mental Health training
91. Character education
92. Diversity and Inclusion forums
93. Wellbeing days/mornings/events
94. Parent open days and information evenings
95. Wellbeing questionnaires
96. Reverse mentoring
97. Daily check ins with a staff member
98. Nurture sessions
99. Risky behaviours education
100. Time-out pass for support or quiet time

It's important to remember when considering the lists that we should not attach provisions to specific conditions. It is never the role of the SMHL to diagnose or speculate on the cause of a condition or what is wrong. Instead, we simply see a child with a need and offer appropriate support.

Ethical dilemmas

In the first chapter, we mentioned the case of Billy, and it would be useful to consider this case again based on the methods of support your school can provide in Tier 1. You may wish to read through it again, and list what could help, both on a formal and informal basis.

Case Study

Billy is 11 and comes to school late most days. You are aware no one at home gets Billy up in the morning or is there to help him get ready for school, and there is no food in the house most of the time. Most nights Billy is awake until the early hours of the morning playing video games. Social care has been involved, but it never reached the stage of any intervention apart from monitoring.

When the school is able to contact mum, she says that Billy can't get out of bed in the morning because he's depressed. Billy has had several sessions with the school counsellor, and there have been improvements in his behaviour, but the punctuality issue remains. Some other members of the form group have also started to be late (but on the surface, they don't seem to have the same challenges at home). When asked about it, they say that Billy always gets away with lateness.

The head of year wants to punish all the students with a

> day in isolation. Do you intervene to change the sanction for Billy?

Sometimes, alongside creating plans of support, the SMHL will have to make tough decisions from which there is a residue of pain: an emotional fallout due to someone or something being impacted negatively. Throughout history, humankind have sought to find ways to solve these moral dilemmas and many ethical theories have evolved as a result. Three that are widely used are deontology, utilitarianism, and virtue ethics.[51]

Deontology

Deontology is a rules-based approach often associated with the 18th-century philosopher Immanuel Kant. The basis of this theory is that moral worth comes from the intention with which an act is carried out and not the outcome. Therefore, people should do the right thing for the right reason. The result is that we should abide by the rules, regardless of outcome, as we followed them with the correct intention. In a practical sense, within a school, we would approach it on the basis that all school rules are there for a reason and should be followed. The problem with this is that there cannot be a rule for every possible scenario (just imagine all the ones you have come across during your career). If we took this approach with Billy's example, we would look at the rules for lateness and respond accordingly, irrespective of his home life, mental health, or safeguarding concerns.

Utilitarianism

Utilitarianism is the approach that seeks the greatest happiness for the greatest number and is attributed to the work of the philosopher Jeremy Bentham and, later on, the 19th-century philosopher John Stuart Mill. The basis of this theory is that the resulting outcome determines moral worth and that people should be free to do as they wish so long as they don't harm others. In a school context, such as Billy's scenario, we would approach it with the intention of the best result for most people and consider removing him from the class. The problem with this approach is that it isn't very concerned with the severity of the impact and does not weigh up the effects or evaluate the possible outcomes for the individual.

Virtue ethics

In its simplest form, virtue ethics is a person-centred often associated in the West with Aristotelian notions of character and virtue. This theory approaches moral evaluations based on cultivating a good character. It relies on *phronesis* or practical moral wisdom, weighing up the virtues in conflict to make a choice (for example, in Billy's case the virtues in conflict might be compassion and fairness). Practical applications in schools would involve making a decision based on the context of the scenario.

If we wanted to approach Billy's dilemma in this way, we might ask the following questions:

1. What needs to be taken into consideration?
2. How does this scenario link to what you value both personally and professionally?
3. Who can help you decide which of these can be prioritised in this situation?
4. What might help mitigate the fallout of this decision?

We may then conclude that we want to act with compassion towards Billy, so we will find a way that he can remain in the class. We also want to consider fairness, as it's not fair to the other children that they're having their learning impacted. So you might discuss this with the colleagues in your team and then perhaps decide that in this situation, it's more important to prioritise compassion over fairness. However, there is no way of judging the situation without taking into consideration all the contextual factors at the time and thinking about what you as the agent value and believe is most important to prioritise.

There is a balance between the values you prioritise on a whole-school level and the values applied by the SMHL to a specific situation. The essence of a moral dilemma is that, unfortunately, there is no way of making this painless for everyone, so the best that can be done in the virtue ethics approach is to prioritise the outcome that feels right and is most aligned to your values and those that are meaningful to the school community. Having regular opportunities to discuss these values and beliefs with colleagues in hypothetical situations will enable more effective deliberation of real issues.

We suggest that, as SMHL, you are more likely to discover the complete picture of what is happening with a pupil if you adopt the virtue ethics paradigm when approaching a school scenario. This is because the other two methods are less concerned with an individual's background and needs. Also, virtue ethics is the only method of the three that can accommodate the other two ethical theories as and when they are appropriate.

Before moving on to the external support available, consider the following questions:

1. How effective is the system of referrals to the SMHL, and does anything need changing or adapting?
2. How will you make this system of referrals available to staff, pupils and parents?
3. How will you approach ethical dilemmas in the future?
4. Who can support you in this?

Summary

✳   A clear school vision is an all-encompassing provision that aids mental health and wellbeing.

✳   The support available is tiered depending on the input level. Tier 1, which is covered in this chapter, is provided by professionals who do not specialise in mental health, i.e., teachers.

✳   A clear threshold between the tiers is optimal, and can be based on recommendations by your local CYPMHS.

✳   Tier 1 interventions can be split into formal and informal, and it is useful to have a list or database of all of these.

✳   Often scenarios will present themselves as ethical dilemmas where someone or something will be negatively impacted by any decision. There are three main ways to approach these types of dilemmas, and we suggest that the virtue ethics approach often works best and is becoming increasingly utilised in education.

Chapter Nine: External Provision

'I think it is really important to know the level of support that is offered and how to access it.'
– H.O. (SMHL, Kent)

The majority of a SMHL's work to support the mental health of students will be within the banks of the school stream. However, they will at times need to access external support after assessing a pupil or exploring all possibilities in the first tier. This is where the SMHL will make judgement calls like those made by the DSL. The question being—is there enough evidence of concern to refer the pupil on?

If the pupil's condition is deteriorating, the school has exhausted all the support they can offer, the pupil poses a serious risk to themselves or others, or their behaviour is consistently problematic at home and/or school, then it is time to refer the pupil onwards into Tier 2 or 3. Consistently problematic behaviour requires a referral to Tier 2, but it must be problematic across both contexts for a Tier 3 referral. To make a referral, a SMHL will have to be familiar with what is available both on a statutory basis and as part of other local offers.

Tier 2

Tier 2 interventions are provided by practitioners who are qualified to deliver mental health interventions. There can be overlap between the 'internal' and 'external' elements of Tier 2, which will depend on whether your school employs an in-school counsellor, for example. If this is the case, the school would have a Tier 2 on-site intervention. However, most schools will have to access Tier 2 support externally.

The term 'practitioners who are qualified to deliver mental health interventions' incorporates more than just counsellors; it includes experts such as art therapists, drama therapists, wellbeing coaches, play specialists, and the Mental Health Support Team (if one has been established in your area). The Mental Health Support Team (MHST) also includes practitioners trained in various therapeutic interventions such as sports and animals, so there is a wide variety of therapeutic possibilities to explore.

In addition to your in-school provisions offered in Tier 1, creating a list of Tier 2 offerings in your area would be valuable. One way of doing this quickly is to work with another school or group of schools to compile the list between you. Your local council may have a directory of services, but if not, the Youth Wellbeing Directory[52] provides a list of organisations from across the UK. There might also be a reference to some of the services available in your local transformation plan.

As well as statutory services, a range of charities support the mental health of children and young people, such as Young Minds, the Anna Freud Centre, Papyrus and Place2Be. There will also be smaller charities in your area that could provide face-to-face support, and it is recommended that you connect with these as soon as possible. As well as their contact details, keep notes of any interactions with the organisation, including the name of the person you dealt with, in case they can help another child in the future. You will need to keep such information secure, in line with your school's GDPR policy.

Once you have an idea of what external support is available, take some time to consider the following scenario and make notes. As we have previously said, there are no right or wrong answers to these ethical dilemmas, so consider it in the context of your own approach and school environment.

Case Study

Ava is thirteen and has had an awful few years after losing her father and grandmother in short succession. The impact on Ava's behaviour has been that she cannot focus on her schoolwork and spends lessons moving around the classroom, distracting other students. Plenty of help has been put in place for Ava, but it doesn't seem to have any effect. Other staff and parents are putting pressure on the head for Ava to be taught outside the classroom, even temporarily. Ava has explained that she draws huge comfort from being with her friends and peers, so her mother is very against this idea. The head comes to you as SMHL and asks you to make the decision. What do you do?

If you have availability in your area, one option to consider is referring Ava to the MHST. This relatively new initiative is not yet available nationwide; there are currently just under 300 teams in place covering 4,700 schools and colleges.[53] New roles called 'Educational Mental Health Practitioners' have been created as part of these teams and are being trained in evidence-based interventions for mild to moderate mental health issues and to advise staff in schools. MHSTs were created to fill the gap before a CYPMHS referral is necessary and to relieve pressure on CYPMHS.[54] Based in a local school, they are an NHS team who support the schools in an area and offer a range of interventions from therapy sessions to training for parents and staff. Most local authorities detail their teams and the schools they serve on their website, and GPs or teachers can make referrals to them. It would therefore be the SMHL who would make referrals on behalf of the school.

If your school isn't currently served by a MHST, but you still require Tier 2 services, this may mean that the school will have to fund the provisions, which must be discussed with the SLT. Ways to reduce this cost could include sharing a counsellor with another group of schools or within a trust. If you go down this route, ensure you seek advice from the counselling regulatory body, the BACP, to make sure the service is evidenced-based, safe, effective, and delivered by qualified and experienced professionals. Always ask a service provider to share their credentials with you. Another suggestion is to make links with a local university to explore options with trainee counsellors towards the end of their studies. There are also online counselling services that you may be able to access, such as Kooth or The Mix. It's important to remember, though, that counselling is not a panacea, and for some pupils, other interventions may prove more effective.

Tier 3

Tier 3 comprises specialist and young people's mental health services. If a student requires referral to Tier 3 or 4 services, this is where the school will need to work in a multi-agency partnership. The SMHL lead will therefore fit into a broader system of support as school partnerships triangulate education, health, and social care. Hopefully, there will be open lines of communication between the different agencies within that partnership.

Within community mental health, there are the following NHS services to support young people:

- Community CYPMHS (formerly CAMHS)
- Early intervention services
- Psychological therapies
- Learning Difficulties CYPMHS
- Eating disorder services
- Gender identity services
- Psychiatric services

Despite there being serious concerns about a child, some behaviour does not indicate a mental health issue and, therefore, may not come under the remit of CYPMHS.[55] Examples of these are:

1. Behaviour that happens in one context, such as only at certain times or towards certain people.

2. When the behaviour is seen as a normal response, such as grieving the loss of a relative.
3. Normal child development, i.e., making choices and learning from them on the road to adulthood.
4. If the child or young person can explain why they are behaving in such a way. An example is when they don't attend school because friends are not attending.

In these cases, alternative interventions should be considered either within the school, local area or online and may involve the family if appropriate. If the student has pupil premium funding, it may be possible to pay for the required services using their allocation. This is particularly appropriate if their issues are impacting their ability to learn, which, when it comes to wellbeing, they invariably are.

Of the above NHS services, CYPMHS is the agency you are likely to have the most contact with within Tier 3. All schools in England have access to NHS Children and Young People Mental Health Services, or CYPMHS (known widely by its former initials CAMHS). It takes referrals of children up to 18 years of age, although in certain places, it may only be up to 16. CYPMHS is a group of NHS-run services that assess and treat children and young people for mental health issues. What is important to remember is that each CYPMHS service works slightly differently, and there is no one model for England. Therefore, it's essential to find out how the service for your local area works, especially concerning their threshold for treatment and how they take referrals.

The SMHL can develop their relationship with their local CYPMHS team by clarifying the referral process with them, including who can refer, what needs to be completed for a referral, and what information needs to be shared. There are, however, certain situations where a referral to CYPMHS should always be made.[56] This is when a child is:

- Developing a significant psychiatric disorder, for example, a psychosis such as schizophrenia or an affective disorder such as significant depression, an eating disorder, obsessive-compulsive disorder, significant anxiety, etc.

- Presenting with significant or escalating self-harming behaviour.
- Presents with symptoms of distress resulting from an event such as abuse, bereavement or divorce that are unusually prolonged or disabling.
- Living with significant family relationship difficulties, which are leading to the child experiencing mental health symptoms.
- Their mental health is seriously impacted by a chronic illness, or their physical health is seriously impacted by emotional difficulties.
- Their capacity to engage in learning and social interactions with peers or adults is significantly reduced due to them exhibiting social communication difficulties, over-activity, impulsivity and a degree of distraction or inattention, which is inappropriate for the child's developmental age.

When applying to CYPMHS, it is important to remember to provide relevant documentation that evidences the behaviour that causes concern, such as a monitoring diary kept by the pupil or a teacher, and evidence of how long it has been happening. Alongside this there should be documentation supporting the impact of the behaviour, such as how the difficulties affect the pupil's day-to-day life and risks to their safety. Finally, it would be best if you also outlined interventions the school has previously taken to address this behaviour and their outcomes.

As CYPMHS is designed to meet the needs of only around 2% of children in your local area,[57] there will likely be referrals that you make that are not accepted. If CYPMHS doesn't accept a referral, they should provide a clear reason for their decision. They should also supply advice on what to do next, including signposting what other local services might best support the child and the most effective things the school and family can do to help them.

Tier 4

Tier 4 relates to inpatient or highly specialised mental health services for conditions such as eating disorders. This will include inpatient CYPMHS, which has multidisciplinary teams including psychologists, psychiatrists, social workers, nurses, psychological therapists, and mental health link workers.

There are few children in most schools needing access to the high-level input of Tier 4 services, but you will come across them occasionally. As SMHL, your role is limited during the time of inpatient care or if the highly specialised services require an absence from school. However, you might need to liaise with the NHS tutors who are trying to continue educating the pupil while in the hospital.

Where your role is essential is when the child returns to school. The adjustments to the school environment the pupil will have to make shouldn't be underestimated, particularly after a long period of inpatient care. It is recommended you meet with the young person or child and their parents before they return to assess their needs and formulate a plan for any required interventions. This would be on the graduated response we discussed in the previous chapter: assess, plan, do, review. The adjustments that may be needed can be wide-ranging and perhaps not things we have previously considered. For example, after months of inpatient care, a young person may struggle with the hustle and bustle of school life, which can be overwhelming. Small things, such as providing a quiet room for them to sit in during lunch or someone to walk through the busy corridors with them between lessons, can make a huge difference.

The way that the school culture approaches the pupil's experiences is also fundamental. On a personal level, they may appreciate having someone they can speak to within the school about their time away. This might help them integrate their experience into their life story rather than it being shrouded in shame or treated as if it never happened.

The SMHL can also help in a broader way by considering how to address potential stigma in the school culture. Stigma is when a person views someone or something negatively because of a distinguishing characteristic or personal trait that's thought to be, or is, a disadvantage. Unfortunately, negative attitudes and beliefs toward people with mental illness are common and can lead to discrimination. In the context of mental health, there are two types of stigmas:

- **Social stigma** includes the negative attitudes and discriminatory behaviours society or particular individuals hold about people with mental health conditions. A belief that *'all people with mental health conditions are violent and dangerous'* is an example of a social stigma.
- **Self-stigma** is when people with mental health problems believe what is being said about their condition, internalise these ideas and agree with these viewpoints, resulting in a feeling of shame or denial. A self-stigma phrase might be, *'I should be able to cope.'*

Part of the role of the SMHL will be to challenge stigma to create an ethos and environment where everyone can thrive. One way to challenge stigma is to provide reliable information through either PSHE or even directly to the pupil or their family, if appropriate.

Monitoring internal and external provisions

As mentioned in the previous chapter, a key part of implementing internal support or provisions is monitoring their effectiveness and making necessary adjustments. This process can be done through either a SDQ or Boxall Profile survey or similar, and reviewing attendance, attainment, and behaviour records. However, often underestimated is the importance of subjective wellbeing—what does the child or young person want to achieve from the intervention? We often forget that subjective elements of feedback are just as important as objective ones and can be simply gathered by asking the pupil how they feel about the intervention. Therefore, monitoring requires clear communication channels between staff, pupils, and parents (where appropriate).

It is just as important to monitor the impact of external provisions, although this is sometimes overlooked. It doesn't have to be a complex procedure; a repeated pupil or teacher survey to monitor the impact on behaviour, attitude, and engagement in school will suffice. We would also hope that the SMHL will receive updates from the external services they engage. This doesn't always happen, so the SMHL might have to request this information and sometimes even push for it. This is important on a case-by-case basis, but also so they can monitor the effectiveness of services, particularly local initiatives. Therefore, the ideal approach is to aim to regularly keep in touch with other agencies to explain your involvement with the child and understand theirs.

When it comes to external provisions, take a moment of reflection to consider the following questions:

1. How would you rate your connections with external agencies, and what could be done to improve these?
2. Are there any additional external support agencies you could explore?
3. How will your school access counselling services?
4. What steps could your school take to reduce stigma surrounding mental illness?

Summary

✳ The internal and external support for mental health and wellbeing are tiered depending on the level of input. Tier 2 interventions are provided by practitioners qualified to deliver mental health interventions. Tier 3 are specialist and young people's mental health services. Tier 4 relates to inpatient or highly specialised mental health services for conditions such as eating disorders.

✳ There are a whole range of Tier 2 providers, and it is a good idea to compile a list of the ones in your local area.

✳ CYPMHS is the predominant service you will access in Tier 3, and it meets the needs of around 2% of children.

✳ The SMHL can help students who have accessed Tier 4 services to settle back into the school environment by addressing potential stigma within the school and looking at interventions that can be made on the pupil's behalf to ease the process of their return.

✳ Monitoring the effectiveness of interventions is essential, which can be done through surveys such as the SDQ or Boxall Profile, reviewing attendance, attainment and behaviour records and seeking feedback from the pupil.

Chapter Ten: The Cycle

'Having the time and space to consider the future of positive mental health in my school is really beneficial and has allowed me to think about the long-term strategic planning and the staff key to its success.'
– D.H. (SMHL, Worcestershire)

In the landscape of mental health and wellbeing in schools, the way we view the island is that it is never a person; instead, it is the SMHL role itself. The terrain can be ever-changing, the school year seasonal, pupils join and eventually move on, but the island, the role of the SMHL, should provide lasting stability. It is a constant that several members of staff may inhabit but not have ownership over. The island should be an enduring feature of the stream, one with a legacy, and we shall share ways to ensure it remains through many cycles of change.

When the island is built upon the foundations of a single member of staff, there is a situation that has the potential to undo all the excellent work a SMHL has fostered during their time in the role and undo the promotion and protection of mental health. The member of staff leaves, and the stability of the island crumbles. People change jobs, retire, go on maternity leave, fall ill, or feel the need to reduce their responsibilities. These events are part of the expected cycle of life. However, the funding currently provided by the DfE is a single payment, and once the school has used this, there is often no additional budget to train another SMHL. The SLT will then have to decide whether to pay for the training again, but from the school's funds, appoint an untrained SMHL or, worst of all, watch as the role slowly dissolves, as does the island that was once a safe port for children and colleagues.

We have been aware of this issue for some time due to the number of SMHLs we speak to around the country. We know of a few schools on their second or third SMHL because colleagues have changed jobs, been required to take a long-term absence, or been on maternity leave. The continuity and sustainability of the role is a potential problem, but one that can be easily accommodated with a few proactive steps.

The longevity of the SMHL role

It is a paradox that the DfE are focused on upskilling a single practitioner when the only way of ensuring longevity in the role is to embed knowledge and practice within the culture of the school and ensure it is disseminated to everyone, including staff, parents, and pupils.

If you have not yet spent all your funding, the sum of £1,200 can often stretch to fund a second SMHL if the first leaves. Several providers, including ourselves, have priced their training to accommodate this. However, as (at the time of writing) the funding is for a single member of staff to be trained, the grant can only be used to upskill the person occupying the SMHL role, and the remainder of the funding would transfer to the new lead on their appointment. In an ideal world, each person who takes over the position will attend a training course, but in some schools, that will not be financially viable. This is part of our reason for writing this book, to help ensure the continuance of the role if you cannot be trained.

The cyclical nature of the academic years and the incremental advances made with each one is key to this. In terms of the academic years passing, it is hoped that from the initial audits of the school, there will be an upward spiral of continuous improvement over the years in terms of the mental health culture and challenging stigma. This progress can then be fed back to staff, pupils, and parents.

The other side to the cyclical nature of the role is the individuals involved committing to passing on their knowledge to the next person to take up the baton. Without this commitment to succession planning, the knowledge learnt through DfE funded training may be lost and potentially not replaced. However, there are a few things the school and the current SMHL can do to prevent this.

First, we recommend that while in the role, the SMHL prepares for a seamless transition in case they must leave without warning (it might be slightly morbid, but we have to plan for all possibilities). Part of this is that all the information from the initial training should be accessible to the new SMHL, whether that is detailed notes or downloaded materials.

Second, we recommend a three-year, three-month, and three-week action plan be put in place to aid the cycle of both the role and its continuity. This means that someone taking over the position can see where the school is and its short, medium, and long-term targets concerning mental health provisions. Ideally, if a small team of people supports the SMHL, the person who takes over the role will have been part of the team and, therefore, know the role, all the information and how to access it. They can then take over the reactive part of the role, dealing with situations as they arise, while they settle into the planning and proactive parts of the position. If the audits and information gathering suggested in the earlier chapters have taken place and been recorded, then the transition will be much smoother.

The additional benefit of having an ongoing plan means that a course has been chartered that can be amended in response to change. Factors such as the demands of the outside world or the cohort of students, mean that the landscape of the school is forever shifting. Anyone who has worked in a school for ten years or more will probably not recognise it from a decade before. Having a three-year plan encourages a SMHL to regularly audit its provisions and assess their impact, which means that as the SMHL, you can navigate this flow and mitigate the impact of change by tweaking accordingly, as required.

Finally, we must warn against the SMHL role becoming insular. If the information the SMHL has garnered (whether through training, audits, future plans, or individual cases) is not accessible to anyone else, there can be undue reliance on one person, and a bottleneck of information can develop, endangering the work. If we think of any other profession requiring strict confidentiality, such as legal matters or medical ones, there are always accessible records in place so another solicitor or doctor can take over if necessary. The same should apply to the role of the SMHL, as it is a *role*, not a person.

If you begin the role and there hasn't been a seamless transition, and there are no records or plans in place, we recommend that you take the steps outlined in the previous chapters to set up the position and approach it as if you are starting again. You can also complete a 'snapshot audit' provided freely by ourselves or a similar service offered by another organisation. While doing this, keep records of your findings and aims and try to build a team around you to ensure the continuous cycle of the role long into the future.

Record keeping

There is a balance to strike between ensuring the longevity of the SMHL role by keeping shared records and ensuring confidentiality is maintained when it comes to the cases of individual pupils or members of staff. The first place to begin is to check with your school how they want to store information in line with GDPR and, you should abide by this guidance. Below is general advice designed to inform rather than supersede your school's GDPR guidance.

As the SMHL, you will have access to information that covers two main categories—personal data and special category data. The former is any information that relates to a living individual, and the latter is highly sensitive data that is afforded extra protection. Much safeguarding and mental health information is categorised as special category data. In the *Guidance for Safer Working Practices* published by the Safer Recruitment Consortium in 2019, there are clear expectations of confidentiality: *'Staff may have access to special category personal data about pupils and their families which must be kept confidential at all times and only shared when legally permissible to do so and in the interest of the child. Records should only be shared with those who have a legitimate professional need to see them... Staff are expected to treat information they receive about pupils and families in a discreet and confidential manner.'*[58]

When deciding what information to share with whom, it may be helpful to bear in mind the government's 2018 *Information Sharing guidance*[59] which sets out 'The Principles' for practitioners working with children to ensure that information is shared using careful judgement. These seven principles are that sharing should be:

1. **Necessary and proportionate**
   When taking decisions about what information to share, you should consider how much information you need to release. Information must be proportionate to the need and level of risk.

2. **Relevant**
   Only information that is relevant to the purposes should be shared with those who need it. This allows others to do their job effectively and make informed decisions.

3. **Adequate**
   Information should be adequate for its purpose.

4. **Accurate**
   Information should be accurate and up to date.

5. **Timely**
   Practitioners should ensure that sufficient information is shared, as well as consider the urgency with which to share it.

6. **Secure**
   Wherever possible, information should be shared in an appropriate, secure way. Practitioners must always follow their organisation's policy on security for handling personal information.

7. **Recorded**

In line with each organisation's own retention policy, the information should not be kept any longer than is necessary.

Therefore, before sharing any special category data, consider if it is necessary to do so, relevant to the person you are sharing it with, adequate for them to do their job of supporting the child, accurate, timely, and shared in an appropriately secure way.

Written information should be deleted or destroyed as soon as it is no longer required, and there should be a way of guaranteeing this will be done before the information is shared rather than leaving it vulnerable to human error. Generally, email systems are not a secure way to share this kind of information, although schools probably use this method widely for logistical reasons. However, specially designed software, such as CPOMS (Child Protection Online Management System), is excellent for ensuring data protection.

If this is not a financially feasible option, you can use password-protected files with links sent via email containing a warning about opening the information out of sight of others. If you retain the primary copy of the file on a shared drive—again, password protected—then you, as the SMHL, have control over when the file is deleted or removed rather than sharing files as attachments that you may lose track of. Perhaps your IT department can support you with the best approach to this in relation to your school's digital infrastructure. Printing off information is not advisable unless you can guarantee it will be stored in line with GDPR by both yourself and the person in receipt of it. We once came across a case of a child's special category data printed off and handed out at a staff meeting, which breached GDPR on multiple levels.

The community

One of the ways to ensure the SMHL role is protected through cycles of change is to develop a supportive network around the school coordinated by the SMHL, but also making links that will benefit the school in the long term. As is the case for any integral and relatively new role, it is important to have a supportive network around you. Connecting with other SMHLs to share good practice, particularly within local areas or between similar school contexts, can be invaluable. If you are struggling with this, we have a group of SMHLs you can join. This is a friendly, supportive community where you can connect with people around the country and share your experience of the role.

If you are taking over the role of SMHL and are perhaps in the process of auditing your school, but wondering whether something requires your immediate attention, we would like to share information on general trends concerning potential gaps. We have gathered this through surveying schools to form a general overview of the mental health and wellbeing landscape within schools. These trends are based on schools that have already begun to address their approach to mental health and are, therefore, likely to be similar to the context of someone reading this book. We will begin with the encouraging results that confirms the excellent work that is already being done, and then move on to potential gaps:

Encouraging results...

⚹ Nearly all the schools openly encouraged staff and pupils to talk about mental health.

⚹ Over three-quarters of schools provided or signposted evidence-based resources for families to develop strategies and skills to support their own mental health needs.

⚹ Most schools worked in partnership with local offers and community services to best serve the mental health needs of pupils.

⚹ Over three-quarters of schools had a clear understanding of the difference between health and education interventions and when they are appropriate.

Potential areas for gaps in policy and provision...

✳ Half of the schools lacked a clear direction for mental health provision that is detailed in their school improvement plan and monitored by governors/the trust.

✳ Half of the schools lacked a clear messaging to the wider community that demonstrates a commitment to reducing stigma surrounding mental health.

✳ Just over half the schools did not have a planned and sustained approach to normalising mental health that is detailed in a policy.

✳ In over half of the schools, staff didn't receive regular training and updates to ensure they have the skills and knowledge to identify mental health concerns in students.

✳ Half of the schools had no mental health policy that cross-references the equality and diversity, the safeguarding, and the behaviour policies.

✳ Only a third of schools thought everyone in the school community was clear about the approach to mental health and mental wellbeing.

✳ Less than a quarter of schools regularly fed back to the pupils about how their involvement has affected policy and practice.

This broad view of general gaps within schools might help draw your attention towards assessing areas that many schools are yet to work on and provide an indication of potential starting points should you find yourself unexpectedly having to pick up the baton.

We are continuing this research and would appreciate your input (there is more about this request in the 'About' section at the end of the book). Evaluating the effect of the SMHL role is complex as we are often dealing with intangibles that are difficult to quantify. Anecdotally, however, it is these intangibles that often have the biggest impact on individual lives. Ultimately, most would agree that the universal aim of education is to prepare young people to become good citizens in a diverse world and mature into individuals who positively impact the local community and wider society. Part of what contributes to this is good mental wellbeing. The things that enrich wellbeing—our thoughts, feelings, emotions, and character—are by their subjective nature difficult to measure, but the intangibility of the results does not make the mission any less worthwhile. As one of our favourite literary voices, Maya Angelou, said, *'I've learned that people will forget what you said, people will forget what you did, but people will never forget how you made them feel.'*

Finally, we would like to thank you for your contribution to bettering the mental health and wellbeing of those within your school community and beyond. It is very probable that there is little space for people to thank you while they are facing sometimes indescribable situations. In ten years', you may be stopped while doing your weekly shop by a former pupil who remembers what you did for them and the difference your actions made. Equally, it may be that they are two aisles away, and you miss each other by moments. That is the serendipitous nature of life. We doubt that you have taken the role for the gratitude. However, it is still comforting sometimes to hear that your work is valuable and valued and this is something important to your own wellbeing, as we all need to feel that we make a difference.

It never ceases to amaze us how much time, energy, and passion the SMHLs we work with pour into this role. We feel privileged to work with a group of individuals so driven by a singular purpose—the desire to do their absolute best for children and communities. As both parents and teachers, we will always be grateful for this.

Summary

✳   To ensure the continuation of the SMHL role, provision should be made to embed it in the school culture, build a team around the SMHL, and keep records that can be accessed by someone taking over the role.

✳   Ideally, each new SMHL will be trained by a DfE-approved provider. If this isn't possible, the knowledge learnt in the SMHL training should be available for other staff members to access.

✳   A three-year, three-month, and three-week plan for mental health and mental wellbeing provision can help with year-on-year improvements within the school.

✳   A SMHL will have access to pupils' and staff members' personal data and special category data.

✳   This data can be highly sensitive, so it should be processed in line with the school's GDPR policy.

The Summary of the Summaries

If you only take 10 things from this book…

1. Mental health, mental wellbeing, and mental illness are related but are **not** interchangeable terms.

   Possible action: Display definitions around the school and build in to PSHE lessons.

2. It is useful to gather pupil and parent perceptions of the school culture and address discrepancies between these views and the views of the school leadership team. Gaps between perceptions of school culture can impact trust and, in turn, trust impacts mental health.

   Possible action: Ask the SLT for a list of statements they believe to be true about the school culture, ideally based around the mission statement or school vision, and survey parents and pupils to see to what extent they agree.

3. Because certain pressure points in a school year are predictable, they can be prepared for, and leadership can look at ways to reduce their impact.

   Possible action: Work with leadership to map out pressure points for staff, implement supportive strategies, and communicate these to staff.

4. An internal or external audit of the whole-school approach to mental health and mental wellbeing can highlight areas that need to be addressed.

    Possible action: Use a tool such as our free Snapshot Audit to highlight which of the 8 areas of whole-school mental health provision you need to focus on.

5. Begin leading by defining your school's best practice approach and choosing several related long-term goals.

    Possible action: Use results from your audit to think about what action steps are needed to move you towards your best practice approach and write long term goals into the SIP.

6. When responding to issues of staff or pupil wellbeing, ethical dilemmas may arise that often do not have a right or wrong answer. It is essential to have a supervisor or team to discuss situations with in confidence.

    Possible action: Set a time to talk as a team about hypothetical scenarios and reflect on how decisions are made.

7. Staff should be trained to identify signs of poor mental health (just as they are trained to identify the signs of potential safeguarding concerns). They should also be aware of risk factors related to developing mental health needs.

    Possible action: Work with SLT to plan regular 5–10-minute training opportunities for all staff during directed time.

8. It is useful to have a list or database of all the Tier 1 interventions offered by your school.

   Possible action: Ask staff to suggest three things they believe support mental health and wellbeing in your school and compile these suggestions into a list that is available centrally.

9. Monitoring the effectiveness of interventions is essential, and can be done through SDQ and Boxall Profile surveys, reviewing attendance, attainment and behaviour records, and seeking feedback from the pupil.

   Possible action: Liaise with SLT about a strategic vision for monitoring and agree an approach that will be reviewed in three months.

10. Ensure there is a robust system for documenting mental health and wellbeing provision/concerns (so that someone taking over the role can access them). Check that systems for sharing information are in line with your GDPR policy.

    Possible action: Speak to the data management lead in your school and inform them of the ways you store and share information to check that these are appropriate.

Notes

Chapter 1

1. Paterson, A. and Grantham, R. (2016) How to make teachers happy: An exploration of teacher wellbeing in the primary school context. Educational & Child Psychology, 33 (2), 90–104

2. Turner, K. and Theilking, M. (2019), Teacher wellbeing: Its effects on teaching practice and student learning. Issues in Educational Research, 29 (3), 938–960

3. Department of Health (2014), *Closing the Gap: Priorities for Essential Change in Mental Health* Accessed online at: https://assets. publishing.service.gov.uk/government/uploads/system/uploads/ attachment_data/file/281250/Closing_the_gap_V2_-_17_Feb_ 2014.pdf

4. NHS England. Accessed online at: https://www.england.nhs.uk/ mental-health/

5. Department for Education (2018). Accessed online at: https://assets. publishing.service.gov.uk/government/uploads/system/uploads/ attachment_data/file/755135/Mental_health_and_behaviour_in_ schools__.pdf

Chapter 2

6. REF: Parliamentary Education Committee (2021). Transcript accessed online at: https://committees.parliament.uk/oralevidence/ 1897/html/

7. NHS (2017) Accessed online at: https://digital.nhs.uk/data-and-information/publications/statistical/mental-health-of-children-and-young-people-in-england/2017/2017

8. Parliamentary Education Committee (2021). Transcript accessed online at: https://committees.parliament.uk/oralevidence/1897/html/

9. Equality Act (2010). Accessed online at: https://www.gov.uk/guidance/equality-act-2010-guidance

10. See https://www.mind.org.uk/information-support/tips-for-everyday-living/racism-and-mental-health/

11. See https://www.gov.uk/government/publications/health-matters-reducing-health-inequalities-in-mental-illness/health-matters-reducing-health-inequalities-in-mental-illness

12. See https://www.gov.uk/government/publications/health-matters-reducing-health-inequalities-in-mental-illness/health-matters-reducing-health-inequalities-in-mental-illness

13. The Story of Gabor Mate – https://opentextbc.ca/abealfreader4/chapter/the-story-of-gabor-mate/

14. Anna Freud Centre 'Looked-after children' https://mentallyhealthyschools.org.uk/risks-and-protective-factors/vulnerable-children/looked-after-children/#:~:text=Because%20of%20their%20experiences%20both, have%20recognisable%20mental%20health%20concerns.

15. See https://www.ons.gov.uk/visualisations/dvc1371/#/E07000223

16. Katherine Weare (2016). *NCB Framework for Promoting Well-being and Responding to Mental Health in Schools*. Accessed online at: https://www.ncb.org.uk/sites/default/files/uploads/files/ncb_framework_for_promoting_well-being_and_responding_to_mental_health_in_schools.pdf

17. Smith TE, Sheridan SM, Kim EM, Park S, Beretvas SN (2020). The Effects of Family-School Partnership Interventions on Academic and Social-Emotional Functioning: A Meta-Analysis Exploring What Works for Whom. *Educational Psychology Review*. 32(2):511-544

Chapter 3

18. Health and Safety Executive. Accessed online at:
    https://www.hse.gov.uk/statistics/dayslost.htm#:
    ~:text=Stress%2C%20depression%20or%20anxiety%20and,
    million%20and%207.3%20million%20respectively.
19. See https://cls.ucl.ac.uk/wp-content/uploads/2020/11/Mental-ill-
    health-at-age-17-%E2%80%93-CLS-briefing-paper-%E2%80%93-
    website.pdf
20. See https://www.hqip.org.uk/resource/report-suicide-by-children-
    and-young-people-2017/#.Y4u373bP1D8

Chapter 4

21. See https://www.youtube.com/watch?v=wLaqdY4SLew
22. See https://assets.publishing.service.gov.uk/government/uploads/
    system/uploads/attachment_data/file/634728/Supporting_Mental-
    health_Case_study_report.pdf
23. See https://assets.publishing.service.gov.uk/government/uploads/
    system/uploads/attachment_data/file/1020249/Promoting_children_
    and_young_people_s_mental_health_and_wellbeing.pdf

Chapter 5

24. Transformational Leadership' Accessed online at: https://www.
    michiganstateuniversityonline.com/resources/leadership/4-is-of-
    transformational-leadership/
25. Katherine Weare (2016). *NCB Framework for Promoting Well-being
    and Responding to Mental Health in Schools*. Accessed online at:
    https://www.ncb.org.uk/sites/default/files/uploads/files/ncb_
    framework_for_promoting_well-being_and_responding_to_mental_
    health_in_schools.pdf

26. University of Cambridge – 'Force Field Analysis' accessed online at
https://www.ifm.eng.cam.ac.uk/research/dstools/force-field-analysis/

Chapter 6

27. Covey, S. R. (1989). The 7 habits of highly effective people: restoring
the character ethic. New York, Simon and Schuster.
28. See https://www.hse.gov.uk/statistics/causdis/stress.pdf
29. See https://www.educationsupport.org.uk/news-and-events/news/
state-of-teachers-health-remains-worrying-despite-emergence-from-
covid-pandemic/
30. See https://www.hse.gov.uk/pubns/indg424.pdf
31. See https://assets.publishing.service.gov.uk/government/uploads/
system/uploads/attachment_data/file/292450/mental-capital-
wellbeing-report.pdf

Chapter 7

32. See https://schoolsweek.co.uk/dfe-schools-get-bigger-as-pupil-
population-increases-by-66000/
33. See https://www.acamh.org/blog/identifying-mental-health-
difficulties-in-children-young-people-the-role-of-schools/
34. See https://www.nice.org.uk/guidance/ng223/chapter/
Recommendations#identifying-children-and-young-people-at-risk-
of-poor-social-emotional-and-mental-wellbeing
35. Faulkner J. Class of 2011 Yearbook: How happy are young people
and why does it matter? [Internet]. Doncaster; 2011 [cited 2017
May 31]. Available from: relate.org.uk
36. Children's Commissioner for England (2015). Protecting children
from harm: A critical assessment of child sexual abuse in the family
network in England and priorities for action [Internet]. London;
[cited 2019 Feb 14].
Available from: childrenscommissioner.gov.uk

37. Barter C, McCarry M, Berridge D, Evans K (2009). Partner exploitation and violence in teenage intimate relationships. Available from: nspcc.org.uk

38. See https://www.england.nhs.uk/wp-content/uploads/2016/02/Mental-Health-Taskforce-FYFV-final.pdf

39. See https://www.england.nhs.uk/wp-content/uploads/2016/02/Mental-Health-Taskforce-FYFV-final.pdf

40. See https://www.england.nhs.uk/wp-content/uploads/2016/02/Mental-Health-Taskforce-FYFV-final.pdf

41. Quoted by Stephanie Tait on Twitter @StephTaitWrites 31.2.2019

42. Natasha Devon MBE | The Mental Health Media Charter

43. Domaradzki J (2021). The Werther Effect, the Papageno Effect or No Effect? A Literature Review. Int J Environ Res Public Health. 18(5):2396. doi: 10.3390/ijerph18052396. PMID: 33804527; PMCID: PMC7967741.

44. See https://www.cdc.gov/violenceprevention/aces/

45. See https://www.corc.uk.net/

46. See https://sdqinfo.org/

47. Law, D. & Bradley, J. Goals and Goal Based Outcomes (GBOs). In: Law, D., & Wolpert, M. (2014). Guide to using outcomes and feedback tools with children, young people and families, pp.129–136

48. See https://new.boxallprofile.org/

Chapter 8

49. Send Code of Practice (2014) https://www.gov.uk/government/publications/send-code-of-practice-0-to-25

50. See http://implementingthrive.org/about-us/the-thrive-framework/

51. See https://plato.stanford.edu/entries/ethics-virtue/

Chapter 9

52. See https://www.annafreud.org/on-my-mind/youth-wellbeing/

53. See https://www.england.nhs.uk/2022/05/nhs-fast-tracks-mental-health-support-for-millions-of-pupils/

54. See https://www.england.nhs.uk/mental-health/cyp/trailblazers/

55. See Sheffield-TaMHS-toolkit.pdf (family-action.org.uk)

56. See Sheffield-TaMHS-toolkit.pdf (family-action.org.uk)

57. See https://mentallyhealthyschools.org.uk/whole-school-approach/camhs/

Chapter 10

58. Professional and Personnel Relationships (cimpress.io). Safer Recruitment Consortium (2019) Guidance for safer working practice for those working with children and young people in education settings.

59. See https://assets.publishing.service.gov.uk/government/uploads/system/uploads/attachment_data/file/1062969/Information_sharing_advice_practitioners_safeguarding_services.pdf

About Dragonfly: Impact Education

During eleven years of teaching together, our professional respect for each other grew into a solid friendship, and we are now what Rachael (citing Aristotle) would call 'character friends'. This means friends who genuinely have each other's best interests at heart and are willing to challenge one another and support each other's growth.

It is on this solid foundation of friendship that we decided to establish Dragonfly: Impact Education. Its formation was based on our belief that what made the most significant difference to children and stayed with them far beyond their school years were the relationships they formed. We wanted to do more to support the whole child by empowering schools to create the kind of culture where children could thrive across the board, both in school and beyond.

We offer several provisions to help with this:

- DfE-approved SMHL training that provides seven hours of training and includes twelve months of support for the SMHL and up to nine additional members of staff.

- Connect Team Membership, where the SMHL and up to nine other staff members from the school join a community of educational professionals and receive six training and networking sessions a year, three resource packs to support mental health, and regular updates about mental health in education.

- A mental health and wellbeing audit (the Four Wing Audit) and support implementing the recommendations in the detailed feedback.

- Bespoke, tailor-made training on a variety of topics.

- One-to-one strategy coaching sessions.

- Supervision and support clusters for SMHLs so they can network with one another.

- A free Snapshot Audit to help new SMHLs assess their school's current provisions (www. snapshotaudit.scoreapp.com)

- A free Facebook group for SMHLs to connect and share best practice (www.facebook.com/groups/wingingitseniormentalhealthleads/)

- Thrive 365, which is a free weekly bulletin offering evidence-based wellbeing tips to share with your whole community.

We also have a small request. We would greatly appreciate your contributions and insights into your SMHL experiences. The government is currently funding this role, but to help ensure its longevity and continued investment, we are gathering information on the impact of the role with the aim of informing policy and practice. This can be done through our website or by sending us an email. Thank you for any contribution of information you can make.

Contact details

Website: www.dragonflyimpact.co.uk
Email: info@dragonflyimpact.co.uk
Facebook: www.facebook.com/dragonflyimpact/
Instagram: www.instagram.com/dragonflyimpact/
Twitter: twitter.com/dragonflyimpact

QR code to connect with us:

Acknowledgements

To our families, we'd like to say thank you for your unwavering support (and patience whilst we worked through many a weekend!).

We'd also like to thank Amy Warren—the best book coach and mentor, without whom this book would never have happened. We're so grateful to both Anna Bird for her time and wisdom as a beta reader, and Rebekah di Palma for her beautiful imagination and artwork—we feel extremely lucky to not only know such talented women, but to be able to call them friends.

Last, but by no means least, a huge and heartfelt thank you to all the senior mental health leads who contributed their insights and experiences to help others.